JIM McLEAN DUNDEE UNITED LEGEND

"By chasing perfection we can catch excellence"
— Vince Lombardi, American Football player, coach and executive.

Production of this book was sponsored by:

Alexander Decorators is a long established Dundee company, delivering a first-class service to private and commercial customers in and around the city. The company is headed up by John Alexander and employs more than 20 people.

John is in the midst of setting up a training centre, Alexander's Community Development, that will help the people of Dundee and surrounding areas. This will be a limited company by guarantee, with charity status.

ALEXANDER'S

Training / Development / Community

Alexander Decorators has been an active supporter of Dundee United Football Club through sponsorship, commercial advertising and corporate events, in association with The Courier and Evening Telegraph. Dundee United FC is an integral part of the city's culture and Alexander Decorators are proud to offer their continued support to the club and the local community, and are very pleased to add their voice to those in this book paying tribute to Jim McLean.

■ **Larkhall Academy team, 1951. Jim is centre, front, with the ball. Of course.**

JIM McLEAN DUNDEE UNITED LEGEND

BY STEVE FINAN

ISBN 978-1-84535-824-2

First published in Great Britain in 2020 by DC Thomson & Co., Ltd., Meadowside, Dundee, DD1 9QJ

Visit **www.dcthomsonshop.co.uk**
To purchase this book.
Or Freephone 0800 318 846 / Overseas customers call +44 1382 575580
Typeset & internal design by Steve Finan.

Cover and back cover design by Leon Strachan.

This book is dedicated to Jim McLean's wife, Doris McLean.

WHILE Jim was giving his time, energy, and footballing brilliance to Dundee United, Doris was there every step of the way supporting him.

Her love and dedication to him has been beyond value. Without Doris, the club wouldn't have had Jim.

In constructing this book, I worked closely with Doris and am grateful for her kind and generous help.

I also interviewed many people who had met Doris over the years. Every single one of them held her in the deepest respect.

On behalf of all Dundee United supporters, thank you Doris.

CONTENTS

OUTSIDE THE GAME

INSIDE THE GAME

ANALYSIS

FAMILY

THE STATUE

IN JIM'S EYES, THE MOST IMPORTANT PEOPLE...

THE PLAY

Introduction, by Steve Finan

THIS book started as one thing, but grew to be another. The intention was to create a football thing, paying tribute to Jim McLean's magnificent achievements. It was to tell the stories of the great games, with the recollections of those who were there to play in them, report on them, or watch them.

But it took on a wider scope, because very quickly the vast breadth of experiences that I found demanded it.

It remains grounded in football, of course, as Jim was himself. But between the lines many other aspects and truths about a complex man leak through. Listen to enough of these tales and you begin to appreciate the effect of one man, a man possessed of a phenomenal strength of character and drive, on his charges, his peers, a football club, an entire city – and how that city's townspeople think of themselves to this day.

Some of the voices belong to people who worked or even lived with Jim McLean every day. Others belong to those who met him once, and even then briefly.

There is a recurring phrase. Jim is described as "ahead of his time". It is only with the long sight granted by several decades that you see how true that is.

Indeed, the Jim McLean era at Tannadice, when looked at in the context of the club's entire history, now seems quite surreal. Were United really that good? Yes, I assure you, they were.

Jim's ability to secure a continent-wide stage for his football club predates the modern rebirth of Dundee, the arrival of the RRS Discovery, the V&A, the Tay Cities Economic Strategy, the renaissance of our city. Jim, ahead of his time again, played a part in laying the foundations for all of that.

Jim made the words "Dundee United" a hot topic on the streets of Barcelona, Rome, Manchester, Monaco, Gothenburg, indeed any city where football is talked about (and that's every European city). Dundonians travelling abroad in the 1980s and '90s became used to discussing their team with everyone they met, because every football fan knew about Dundee United.

Allow me, by comparison, to mention the town of Neuss (it's not far from Monchengladbach). It has a population roughly 10,000 more than Dundee. Its football club, VfR 06 Neuss, plays in the Nordrhein-Westfalen Bezirksliga, a regional league in Germany. When did you last discuss 06 Neuss in the pub? Or the teams of Lleida in Spain, or Rybnik in Poland, or Peterborough in England? They are all towns of similar size to Dundee. No team from these places has ever qualified for a European competition, far less experienced the media circus of making it to a final.

Jim's achievements threw a limelight on oor toon. The final, beamed to hundreds of millions of households, showed how sporting Dundonians were. If you think such publicity comes easy, then you are naïve. Cities beg for that sort of recognition. Ask any Peterbourian.

This book works towards its final chapter, which deals with Phil Differ's stage play about Jim, *Smile*, and will serve to represent the conclusion of the tributes. A fitting endpoint, I hope, because summing up Jim is what the play itself intended to do.

Me? I'm just a United fan who reckoned that if anyone from my home town deserved a book to celebrate their achievements, then it must be Jim McLean.

I'd grown up in the 1970s, as United steadily got better and better, with steadfast truths in my world: the sun rose in the morning, my mother was to be obeyed, and Jim McLean was in charge of Dundee United.

By 1983 I had become used to the Tangerine Dream Machine winning trophies regularly and producing excellent football every week, with half the team made up of Scottish internationals.

This was good.

Then John Greig resigned as manager of Rangers and they made an offer to oor Jim to become their boss.

This was awful.

Football fans become used to players moving on. Andy Gray had gone to Aston Villa, which was painful, and my father often mentioned how terrible it had been when Hurricane Hutch left Tannadice for Newcastle.

But Jim, the man who stopped our players drifting off to other clubs easily, couldn't walk out on us could he? Would he? He's from Larkhall. Which team did he support as a boy? How much cash were they offering?

Something radical had to be done.

Luckily, Breeks at Grouchos was of a similar mind and had badges produced saying: "Jim Don't Go" and "McLean Must Stay".

One sounded a little like pleading, the other was a more strident demand. I couldn't make up my mind which of these tones to adopt, so bought one of each. I still have them.

Jim, obviously aware of the pins on my black-and-tangerine-barred scarf, decided Ibrox wasn't for him.

I was very pleased.

Jim's actions spoke of that rarest of things, loyalty. And of finishing a job you started. He demonstrated that there are some things that just can't be bought.

Those are life lessons.

In my formative years, football meant everything to me. I was, and still am, obsessed. If Jim had gone to Rangers in '83 I don't think there would have been a Roma semi-final (cursed be their name) or Gothenburg final (nice lads those Swedes, even if they did beat us).

This book tells many stories of Jim, from many sources. Some you might have heard, though several will surprise you. Some, I very much hope, will bring back poignant memories and good memories.

Yes, those of us who lived through the McLean era at United can evaluate it with better clarity now a few years have passed. I just didn't appreciate it enough at the time. None of us did.

Above all, this book is an expression of gratitude to Mr McLean for making my experience of being a young football fan – and thousands of Arabs like me – an adventure we'll never forget.

Thanks Jim.

Foreword, by Tom Duthie

FOR a provincial club, Dundee United's history has been laced with more than its share of big names. Even back in the days when success at Tannadice was often defined as just survival as a club, United boasted some interesting figures, not least in the shape of three-times manager Jimmy Brownlie, a Scottish international goalkeeper who was one of the big names of the early part of the 20th Century.

In more recent times, as the success of the team on the park gathered pace, United teams boasted names like Ron Yeats, Doug Smith, Orjan Persson, Andy Gray, Dave Narey, Paul Hegarty and Paul Sturrock. They were men who earned legendary status at Tannadice and beyond during illustrious careers.

Likewise, the success of managers such as Jerry Kerr, Ivan Golac, Craig Levein and Peter Houston means they are names the club is proud to be associated with.

And it should not be forgotten that two of the best football brains Scotland produced in the latter part of the last century, Walter Smith and Archie Knox, picked up a fair chunk of their game knowledge while employees of the Tangerines.

Those are illustrious lists, of that there is no doubt. But anyone who knows anything about Dundee United would have to agree there is no question over which single figure in the club's history stands out more than any other.

Way more, in fact. And the calibre of the names just listed shows how special this man was to United.

He is, of course, Jim McLean, who took Dundee United to the kind of heights no one at a club of its size could have previously dreamed about and whose shadow, even today, some 27 years after he retired as manager, still looms large at Tannadice.

The work he did in 22 years as team boss set the standards that every United team to this day is judged by. Tough as it may be, that's something that will not, and should not, change.

When it comes to football knowledge, it is no exaggeration to say in their 111-year history the Tangerines have never seen his like. It is no slight on any future manager to add they are unlikely to ever again.

To describe Jim McLean as a genius is neither praise nor hyperbole. It's a statement of fact.

His record shows that. He took the club he himself described as no bigger than a corner shop to a Scottish title, two League Cups, a European Cup semi-final and the final of the UEFA Cup.

It's impossible to imagine those last two achievements happening again at United or any other club of a similar size. But possibly McLean's biggest strength was consistency of performance, no better example of which is the fact he led his teams to European qualification in every season bar one between 1974 and 1991.

On top of all that, his ability to produce talent of the very highest class over a period of not just years, but decades has, perhaps, never been rivalled by any other Scottish manager.

Players like Dave Narey, Paul Sturrock, Andy Gray, Duncan Ferguson and Maurice Malpas all came through the youth ranks at United and would go on to be the envy of big clubs well beyond the borders of the Scottish game. Indeed, it's fair to say had their careers come a decade or two later, they would have been sold on not just for millions, but tens of millions.

Turning to the great man's relationship with the media, there can be no hiding the fact it was turbulent. At times very turbulent.

He made mistakes, some big and well-publicised, and of that there is again no question. But what has been largely forgotten is he had an understanding of the media and its value like few other managers have ever had.

His labelling of his beloved United, for instance, as "a corner shop" was a masterstroke that guaranteed extensive publicity of their achievements when jousting – another word he used well elsewhere – with the hypermarkets of the Scottish and European game.

And whatever his frustrations with reporters who wouldn't always write stories the way he wanted them to, he made the most of performances on the park to make sure United got the kind of publicity they deserved.

That was to the benefit of his club and you can be sure his astute use of newspapers and broadcasters was a factor in zeroes being added to the sponsorship contracts United gained during his time both as chairman and manager.

His public utterances about the Press may not always have been complimentary, but he knew that consistently getting Dundee United a prominent place on the back pages was a good thing.

Accordingly, he would meet local football writers on a daily basis and provided a steady flow of good hard copy that made sure the Tangerines were never far away from the limelight.

He, of course, knew the best way for his team to get attention was through their results on the park and that was where his true genius lay.

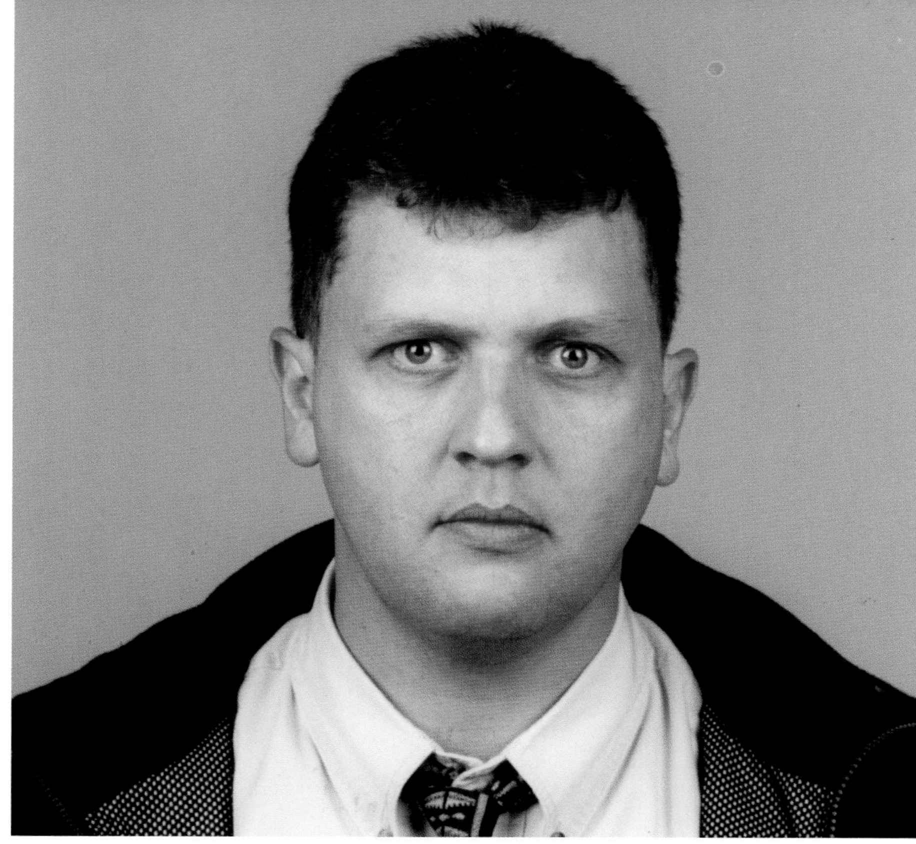

■ Tom was chief sports writer with The Dundee Evening Telegraph throughout Jim McLean's glory years. This what Tom looked like when he started the job all those years ago.

Over his 22-year tenure as manager at Tannadice, he had a win rate of just over 48%. That is quite exceptional given he was in charge for 1160 games.

Add to that the trophies and European successes, plus countless other great days for United fans, and it's no wonder why to this day the name James McLean is revered by Dundee United fans.

So, who is he?

TALE OF THE TAPE: PLAYER AND MANAGER.

JAMES YUILLE MCLEAN was born on August 2nd, 1937, the second of three sons to Tom, a baker, and Annie McLean. He was born in Larkhall, but raised at No. 6 Douglas Drive, a four-in-a-block council house of a type once widespread in Scotland, in the nearby village of Ashgill.

His father had been a good junior footballer, and was provisionally signed to Hearts at one point. His grandfather, William Yuille, played for Rangers before World War 1.

Jim's brothers Willie (born 1935) and Tommy (1947) were also successful professional football players and managers. Tommy was capped for Scotland.

Jim was an inside-forward and played junior football for Stonehouse Violet, then Larkhall Thistle, while also serving an apprenticeship as a joiner, before becoming a league player with Hamilton Academical in 1956.

He played 129 games for Accies, scoring 57 goals.

He then signed for Clyde in 1960, for a transfer fee of £5,000, playing 102 games for The Bully Wee and scoring 32 goals.

■ **Jim playing for Clyde.**

His first full-time contract as a footballer came in 1965, when he joined Dundee for a fee of £10,000. He played 90 games for the Dark Blues, scoring 28 goals.

Jim was transferred to Kilmarnock in 1968, playing in the same team as Tommy, while Willie was a coach at the club. Jim played 56 games for the Rugby Park club, scoring seven goals.

In 1970, still living in Dundee although playing for Killie, Dundee FC manager John Prentice (who had also been his manager at Clyde) approached him to become a coach at Dens Park.

He gave up playing, after 377 games as a pro, having scored 124 competitive goals.

He remained as coach to Prentice, a man Jim regards as his mentor, until, in December 1971, he took the job as manager of Tannadice and changed the face of football in the city of Dundee.

Jim was manager of Dundee United until 1993, then became chairman and managing director. He led United into 1117 competitive games, winning 534 of them, losing 314 and drawing 269.

But mere statistics do not capture the full story.

Dundee United had always had potential, and Jerry Kerr had done much to drag them out of the dark days of the 1950s, when United regularly grubbed about the bottom of the old Second Division.

Jim took them to glory. He won the League Cup in 1979, United's first ever senior trophy, then repeated that feat a year later with a 3-0 demolition of local rivals Dundee.

In 1982-83, however, Jim pulled off one of the most remarkable feats in the history of Scottish football.

If the greatest ever achievement by a Scottish club is Celtic's capture of the 1967 European Cup with 11 players born within a few miles of Celtic Park, then Dundee United winning the Premier League using not much more than 14 players (10 of whom had come through the club's youth system) must stand second.

Jim then took United on a run to the semi-final of the 1984 European Cup, before getting to the final of the UEFA Cup in 1987.

Though United have long since overtaken Dundee FC to become the bigger club in the city, Jim's start-point when creating a European powerhouse was with a club that was the second largest in its city, and that city being the fourth largest in its country, and that country being the 29th largest in Europe. Such clubs should not be able to do the things Jim made United achieve. No other club from such a humble start-point has ever done so, or probably ever will again.

Under Jim McLean, Dundee United qualified for European competition in most of Jim's seasons in charge, including 14 qualifications in a row from 1977-78.

United reached six Scottish Cup Finals under Jim, and four League Cup Finals, winning two. Apart from the wartime cup of 1940, Dundee United had never contested a national final until Jim arrived.

The club had never had a player capped for Scotland until one of Jim's academy graduates, David Narey, won the first of his 35 caps in 1977.

Jim McLean was inducted into the Scottish Football Hall of Fame in 2005.

Proud of the standards Jim set

TRIBUTE: WALTER SMITH.

WALTER SMITH OBE joined United, aged 18, in 1966 and played (apart from a couple of seasons at Dumbarton) until 1980, before becoming assistant manager.

He played 183 games for United, mostly at right-half or as a central defender, scoring 17 goals — including the winner in a derby at Dens in September 1973.

He left Tannadice to become assistant at Rangers in 1986, recruited to provide detailed knowledge of Scottish football to the incoming Graeme Souness.

Walter took over as Rangers manager in 1991 and presided over one of the most successful eras in Ibrox history.

But it is as assistant-manager and then as fellow board member to Jim McLean, that he is remembered at Tannadice. Few people knew Jim, and how he thought, how he worked, as well as the man who spent years beside him in the dug-out, Walter Smith.

In Walter's own words:

"I don't think it was a huge surprise when Jim arrived at Tannadice in December '71.

"At that time, there wasn't the same situation that there is today – namely, get a few bad results and you are liable to be sacked.

"Jerry Kerr had done well with United over a period of time, bringing the team up from the bottom of the old Second Division and establishing them in the top flight while also improving both the playing squad and the stadium.

"But he moved on to be general manager, leaving a vacancy which Jim filled.

"Jim was obviously a good bit younger than Jerry, and making a name for himself up the street. He was a bit more modern in his thinking and his approach, which was to be expected.

"Jim also had his own ideas which obviously rubbed off on some. I was only in my early 20s then, and still playing, but seeing someone like Jim, who was also still relatively young, sparked my own interest in coaching.

"Around that time there were a number of coaches in Scotland who had started out in management as younger men, maybe with fresher ideas; Eddie Turnbull would have been one a few years before, as he brought through a good Aberdeen team, and then of course there would have been another in Sir Alex Ferguson.

"United's fitness work changed, training changed,

■ **April 1974. Jim and Walter are presented with the set of strips United would wear in the club's first Scottish Cup Final by Jim Paton of Bukta.**

there was a change in focus, tactically. Modern techniques came in to play, but some of the biggest changes were taking place off the pitch.

"Jim identified the need for a youth policy, with a robust scouting network, both locally and around the major centres, identifying the talent initially, then allowing the coaches at the club to give those players a chance to progress, in United's case, all the way through to the first team.

"All instigated by Jim McLean.

"It was going to take a few years for those policies to come to fruition, but slowly, the older, established players in the team made way for the younger men. There was a transformation in personnel, and performance levels.

"We reached the Scottish Cup final in 1974, and there was a steady improvement in that team and group of players which would eventually win and retain the League Cup, and reach another Scottish Cup final.

The very nature of being a provincial team meant you were always likely – as a great many teams did at that time – to lose your best players to clubs in England. It happened with Andy Gray, and the likes of Ray Stewart.

"Those were big-money sales, however money was still tight, though Jim made some astute signings to augment the core of players who had come through our own infrastructure, such as Dave Narey, Graeme Payne, Paul Sturrock and Davie Dodds.

"Paul Hegarty, signed from Hamilton Accies, was one of the players we bought, Eamonn Bannon arriving from Chelsea for a record fee was another.

"It was maybe a measure of Jim's eye for talent that he saw something in Paul, signed as a striker, and decided to convert him in to a centre-back – and

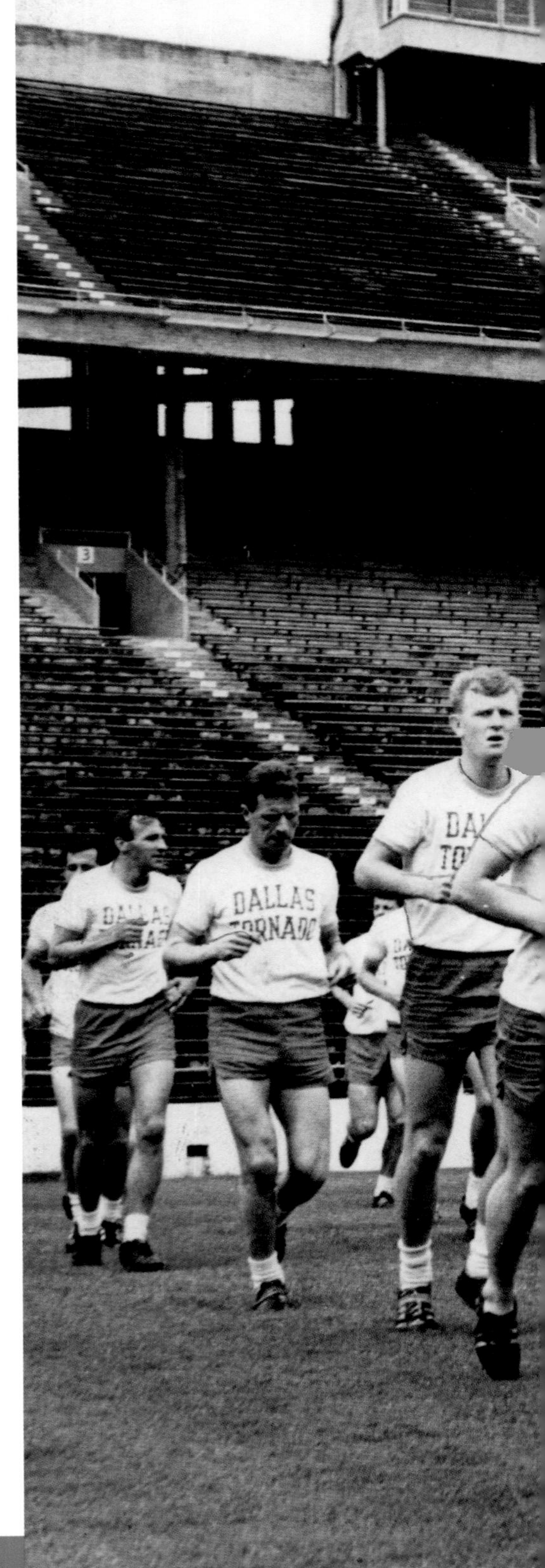

June 4th, 1967. United played 11 games to promote football in the USA under the name Dallas Tornado. Walter was one of the United players who travelled. This training session was at the Cotton Bowl, Dallas. The visible players are, from left: Tommy Millar, Doug Smith, Finn Seemann, Jackie Graham, Dennis Gillespie, Walter and Billy Hainey.

DALLAS

it was a very successful transformation, you would have to say.

"By the time the '82-83 season came around, the likes of Richard Gough, Ralph Milne and Maurice Malpas were all established players.

"When you reflect on that team, we didn't use many players; they were all physically fit, always ready, and hungry, and we didn't suffer badly with suspensions either. We picked our best players and they were ultimately up to the challenges encountered and the ambitions set.

"In the space of a dozen years, United had gone from mid-table to champions, and that progression, to ultimately land the biggest competition in the country, was fashioned and driven by Jim McLean.

"Do I think he got the credit he deserved at the time? I think if you look at the clubs who have been Scottish champions since then – other than a couple of titles an excellent Aberdeen side won directly after United – it has been dominated by the Old Firm.

"United's winning season was maybe viewed then as part of the club's progression. Looking at it today, nearly 40 years on, it is even more remarkable. So, you could say Jim's biggest achievement was perhaps lost in the moment.

"Of course, football is entirely binary; you win or you lose. A win is viewed as success, defeat failure. Black and white. But that is unfair; the reality is that it's never that simple.

"Jim, and United, in terms of silverware could have

■ December 8th, 1973. Walter has words with the ref during a blizzard-hit 3-3 draw at Celtic Park.

landed an even bigger prize, the ultimate in European club football the following season, but it wasn't to be.

"That's really where I think, historically, Jim might not have achieved the acclaim he truly merited, taking a Scottish provincial club to the semi-final of the European Cup. You could make an identical case a few years later in the UEFA Cup.

"Perhaps, we were a touch naïve, a bit raw and inexperienced that day in Rome. And, because we lost, it is viewed as a failure, rather than what I will always believe was an extraordinary achievement, both by the manager and that group of players. To defeat Roma, with all their resources and talent, at Tannadice, and get so close to the final was incredible.

"I know, Jim was massively disappointed, as were the players, naturally. However, all these years on, and seeing what other Scottish clubs have done since, United's run stands out more than we perhaps appreciated fully at the time.

"That might also be said of Jim McLean, the manager, the coach.

"Remember too, that while he was steering United to the

August 6th, 1985. Walter in his last full season at Tannadice, Back, from left: Davie Dodds, John Clark, Billy Thomson, Hamish McAlpine, Richard Gough, Dave Beaumont. Middle Jim McLean, Derek Stark, Gary McGinnis, Dave Narey, Stuart Beedie, Tommy Coyne, Gordon McLeod, John Holt, Bill Ramsay (physio). Front: Walter, Maurice Malpas, Ralph Milne, Billy Kirkwood, Paul Hegarty, Paul Sturrock, Eamonn Bannon, John Reilly, Gordon Wallace (coach).

VG

top, Mr Stein (Jock Stein) as Scotland manager, asked Jim to be his assistant at international level.

"As a coach, it is a tremendous accolade to be asked to fulfil such a role. That it was Mr Stein who invited him to be his No.2, was also a measure of everything Jim was as a coach of the highest standing. He deserved it, and I know he enjoyed that experience, and what he gleaned from it.

"When you set out in management, you do pick up tips and traits from those you have worked with, but ultimately you will be your own man. That was something Jim McLean was throughout his entire career as United manager.

"He was never the type to overly celebrate, or show his emotions, publicly at any rate. But he was immensely proud of the job he had done, and in particular of the standards he had set.

"Jim did it his way.

"You cannot replicate that drive, determination, ambition, or intensity. I was very fortunate to work with him for a number of years, and play a wee part in what he achieved at United.

"His achievements tell you he is one of the best Scottish club managers, ever. To do that with Dundee United, makes it all the more notable. He did it his way, in a playing sense on the field, and in how he managed the club.

"Not only was it his way, it was the right way for him."

Walter and Jim on that great day at Dens Park, May 14th, 1983.

Maurice, have you no ambition?

TRIBUTE: MAURICE FRIEL, FORMER DUNDEE FC PHYSIO.

MY first association with Jim "Beano" McLean was when we were both at Dens in 1970, with John Prentice as our manager.

When Jim became United manager he called me up to scout for players for him "doon in the West."

He told me, "We have nae money, but if we can manage to stay up this season we could all right."

What an offer! How could I refuse?

The McLean Magic had started – the rest is history.

We did stay up, and went up and up! The successes just kept coming.

Several years later, in 1977, I was approached by two leading English clubs to do a similar job for them.

Because of their respect for Jim and Dundee United as a football club, both of the English outfits insisted that l clear the matter with Jim before making my choice.

"Why do you want to join either of them when you've already got us?" exploded Jim when I told him.

"HAVE YOU GOT NO AMBITION?"

Incidentally, the choice I had was between working for Arsenal or Manchester United.

Even then, Jim was punching his above his weight, as equals with the big boys.

Nowadays, when I think of Jim McLean I'm thinking – WHA'S LIKE US? GAE FEW!

Author's note: I had to ask Maurice (who is fondly remembered by Dundee supporters as a very nice bloke and skilled, and incredibly fast when running on to treat a player, physio) about the "Beano" nickname.

Maurice explained: "Jim was a player at Dundee at the same time as George McLean, the ex Rangers centre-forward, whose nickname was 'Dandy' It was a connection with DC Thomson comic figures of the Dandy and Beano comics. Davie Johnston was known as 'Biffo'."

■ Right: Jim as coach of Dundee FC. He would cherry-pick several members of this team to eventually join him at Tannadice as players, backroom staff or scouts.

It is a telling measure of the high regard these men retained for their former coach that late on the night of Dundee FC's League Cup win in December 1973 – fully two years after Jim had left Dens Park – the celebrating Dundee players ended up at Jim and Doris's house in Broughty Ferry, with the cup and some carry-outs.

Maurice Friel recalls it as "quite a night".

■ Back, from left: Bobby Wilson, Iain Phillip*, Mike Hewitt, Ally Donaldson, George Stewart, Davie Johnston, Jim himself*. Middle: Jim's mentor and good friend John Prentice, Bobby Robinson*, Ian Scott, Jim Steele, Ron Selway, Duncan Lambie, physio Maurice Friel*. Front: Alex Bryce, John Duncan, Alex Kininmonth, Doug Houston*, Gordon Wallace*, Jocky Scott, Jimmy Wilson.
* Denotes that these men were chosen to join Jim at United.

This was the Tannadice that Jim inherited. A wee club, a wee support, a decent but basic stadium.

But laurels aren't given for where you start, they are awarded for what you achieve.

Everything about Dundee United was better off for Jim McLean's attentions. The crowds, the club's standing in the game, the stadium, and the list of successes.

Dundee United had always been a club with potential. The directors who brought Jim to the club, to realise that potential, should be given the highest of praise for making an excellent decision.

Jim made Tannadice his own.

SKOL
LAGER
HIRE
Betty White
Make it a habit!
ABBOTS

Creating lifelong United supporters

FAN TRIBUTE: KIERAN MALONE, DUNDEE.

I MET Jim when my son Brendan was six and a member of the Young Lions supporters club. At that time, kids were chosen to be mascot at random from the Young Lions and Brendan drew the first home game of the season, against Hibs, August 17th, 1997.

It was a sunny Sunday, and the game was shown on Sky TV. We were taken to the boardroom and welcomed by a really nice woman who we later found out was Doris, Jim's wife. She told us Jim would be with us soon.

I have to be honest, like many others, I had an image of Jim Mclean as a man not to be messed with, and lacking a sense of humour.

However, the man that walked in couldn't have been further from the fearsome reputation. He introduced himself and his entire focus from that point was Brendan, the day's mascot.

Jim was lovely, he walked us round the boardroom, introduced the mascot to everyone there.

He pointed out everything to Brendan. He shared stories of United's history, of all the photos, trophies and memorabilia. He showed us his office and Brendan even sat in his chairman's chair.

We then got a tour of Tannadice, with Jim as guide. It was amazing to see him lead Brendan round and hear the conversation between them. Jim took time, answered all his questions, and made him smile and relax.

Jim was patient, kind and happy to chat to a curious six-year-old.

He then took us to the dressing room to meet the players. Erik Pedersen was kicking stuff about the floor, shouting and geeing everyone up, saying "Let's get into these b****".

But Jim gave him a telling off for speaking like that in front of the mascot.

I thanked Jim for his time and the way he had treated Brendan. Jim replied simply that youngsters were more important than anything. They would either grow up to play for the club, or become supporters and stay for life.

As he was about to leave Jim turned to Brendan and thanked him for being mascot and said he was to use his office to get changed to watch the game.

If anyone said anything to him he was to tell them: "see Jim McLean".

Brendan replied "OK Jim" like he was speaking to his best friend, and Jim chuckled and beamed the biggest smile.

Jim was right. Brendan didn't quite make it as football player, but he has remained a loyal United supporter to this day.

Unique

FAN TRIBUTE: ROSS FORBES, ALBERTA, CANADA (FORMERLY OF FINTRY).

I WAS privileged to witness Jim McLean succeeding Jerry Kerr and transforming Dundee United with his unique understanding of how to play the beautiful game.

Jim built a succession of teams, incorporating the right blend of youth and experience, to eventually conquer Scottish and European football and put my wee team, Dundee United, on the global football map.

To me, he will forever be a legend.

This photo of Jim, with long-time friend, coach, trainer and physio Andy Dickson (who was himself manager of Dunfermline FC for five years, 1955-60) was taken in December, 1971. It is thought to be Jim's first full training session as Dundee United boss.

Jim the young football player

TRIBUTE: WILLIE McLEAN, JIM'S BROTHER AND A RESPECTED PLAYER AND MANAGER IN HIS OWN RIGHT.

JIM McLEAN'S best years as a player probably came during his time with Clyde, roughly the period between 1961 and 1965.

Jim was an inside-right. As his brother Willie puts it, "Jim was right-footed, I was left-footed, but bloody Tommy was two-footed. The young anes aye get a' the luck!"

As an inside-right, Jim would usually play with a number 8 on his back. In those days, teams played the 2-3-5 formation but the inside-forwards were slightly withdrawn, instead of the flat front five the formation suggests.

"They used to term it a W-M formation. the inside forwards played as the bottom points of the W, supporting the wingers and centre-forward. Nowadays, Jim would have been termed an attacking midfielder.

Willie says he was a very good distributor. "The nearest I could do for someone to compare him to was Ian McMillan, a legendary passer of the ball who I'd played with at Airdrie, before he was transferred to Rangers. They used to call him 'The wee prime minister'. He made it all tick.

"Ian used to say: 'When I get the ball, Willie, you start running'. I'd ask, 'But where will I run to?' and Ian would reply 'It doesn't matter, just run and I'll find you with a pass.' And he would. He'd put a pass through between the full-back and centre-half and I'd be in on the goalie.

"Jim was just like that. Even back in those days he firmly believed in his team keeping the ball, so he didn't lump it up the park, he wanted to play passes.

"He was very good with a dead ball too, a lot of his goals, and he got quite a few, were from dead-balls. He took a good penalty too. He struck the ball very well, that's what all these dead-ball experts can do. It's about making a good connection with the ball."

"Jim's manager at Clyde, and then Dundee, was big John Prentice. John and oor Jim thought the same way about the game. Big John loved him, and built that Clyde team around Jim's passing.

"They finished seventh in 1964-65, a place above Celtic. They'd been fourth for a good few weeks of that season too. Not bad for a part-time team. Jim and Sam Hastings had a great understanding. Sam was the left winger and Jim would feed him the ball.

"They had a very strong team in those days, Harry Glasgow at the back, Jim Fraser, Davie Souter – all good players.

"Harry Haddock, the left-back was especially good at

■ From Doris McLean's collection of photos, Willie (left) and Jim playing for Larkhall Thistle.

taking the ball down and passing it out from the back. He was a hell of a player, got a few Scotland caps too. Great servant to Clyde.

"He would have been a good bit older than Jim, mind. Harry was the captain. He probably retired during Jim's time there. But Jim would have looked at how he went about playing the game and been a part of the moves that they put together on the left-hand side.

"That's what made Clyde such a good team. They always passed the ball very well. They played football on the deck which, believe me, wasn't easy on Shawfield in those days. It was a very tight pitch and worn and bumpy.

"It was more of a dog track with a football pitch rather than a football venue.

"They used to walk the dogs up and down the grass between the races at night, so the next day you had to watch where you put your feet, and definitely be careful if you were going down for a sliding tackle!

"Big Prentice wanted to do the same at Dens as he had at Clyde, build a team around Jim. And base it all on passing the ball, keeping the ball. Neither of them ever wanted to give the ball away cheaply. I don't think Prentice was at Dens long enough with Jim or really got the players to make it work. You have to have a set of like-minded players to make that type of football work.

"Dundee never really got the best out of Jim as a player, or as a coach. It could have all been very different at Dens Park."

As brothers always are, Willie, Jim, and Tommy were highly competitive with each other – though especially the two older brothers just two years apart (Tommy is 10 years younger).

"We all wanted to win," Willie says. "We'd learned the game on the streets together, played for the same teams, played for the same school.

"When I was at Larkhall High School we won the Scottish Intermediate Shield, it was for laddies aged under 15. But Jim, two years younger – his team got knocked out in the semi-final of their year. I certainly didn't let him forget that!

"It was the same if we played each other in the senior game. We'd do anything to win.

"We got it from our dad. He was the hardest man to please. According to our dad, as a laddie playing schools or junior football, I never once had a good game. Neither did Jim. Though I'd just say 'Aye dad, aye' when he was pointing out my mistakes. Jim was more argumentative, he'd give it right back to our dad. I'd put my head in my hands knowing we'd be there all night once they got going. They were more volatile than me, the two of them. Very alike in that.

"That photo you have of Jim's school team, though (see frontispiece). It was a good team. One of the other laddies, and I can't remember which one, would be Tommy Ewing, he was in Jim's year at school and played for Larkhall Thistle too.

"He went on to play for Partick and Aston Villa down south. He got a couple of Scotland caps too. Very good left-winger. Oor Jim's sitting with the ball and the cup

■ Jim in Clyde's line-up, 1962. Back, from left: David White, Moffat, John Finnegan, Harry Haddock, Tommy McCulloch, Donnelly, Dan Currie, Bobby Veitch. Middle: Danny Malloy, Willie Finlay, John McHugh, Tommy Burke, Dick Grant, Jim McLean, Willie McCulloch, Davie Thompson. Front: Graham McFarlane, John McLaughlin, John Divers, Bobby Steel, Ian Blair, John Colrain.

at his feet in that photo, though. You can see who's team that was!

"But our father never used to come and watch us when we played in the senior game. He would say there was no way to win. If one brother won, the other lost, and he wouldn't take a side. He was hard, but he was very, very fair. You can see where Jim gets that in his personality too.

"Though I do remember we all went to see Tommy play for Killie in that famous Eintracht Frankfurt game at Rugby Park in 1964. Me, Jim and my father standing on the terraces getting soaked. No complimentary tickets in those days, we paid to get in. Great game, though. The Germans were 3-0 up from the first leg, and scored right at the start of the game over here. But Killie came back to win 5-1 on the night, 5-4 on aggregate. It was a great European night, I reckon Jim might have learned a bit about European football from that one.

"Our father did everything he could to help us be footballers. He worked night-shifts at a bakery in Hamilton, then drove a taxi and sometimes buses during the day so that we could have boots and shin guards and didn't have to go down the pit age 15. He worked all hours and made sure we were raised properly.

"He showed us what hard work was. None of us ever forgot that."

So was Jim always a good player, right from when he was a wee boy?

"Aye, you could see what he was," says Willie. "We played for Larkhall Academy, but Jim was never involved much in juvenile football. He went straight from schools football to playing junior. Schools football was very, very big in those days. He stood out as a good player even then.

"We all played football in the street, and anywhere that was big enough to put jerseys down for goals. All day every day. Every laddie did. That's where Jim learned the game. Ashgill was a wee village, but Larkhall was a big village."

Jim and Willie teamed up off the field too.

"Jim was a joiner and I was a draughtsman, I served my time in an office in Wishaw," Willie said. "So we planned out and built a wee street of eight houses in Ashgill. They are still there today. Jim did the building."

What about when you were opposing managers?

"I did 12 years as a manager, and played Jim's teams many a time. When I was at Motherwell, Jim would phone up at lunchtimes and ask how our training had gone that morning. What we'd tried, what had worked, what hadn't worked. We'd talk about it.

"Then I'd ask what he'd been doing at training and he'd say 'Aw, nuthin much'. He'd never give anything away about what he was doing. I used to tell the lads to say I wasn't available when he phoned in the run-up to us playing United. It was just Jim looking for wee ways to get information on how we might play. The competitiveness never stopped.

"I'd go up to Tannadice to watch United's big European games, though. I'd want to beat Jim's teams if we played against them, but Dundee United doing well in Europe was good for all the clubs in Scotland.

"Aye, Jim had a good team to watch."

Jim formed a potent left-sided attack for Clyde with winger Sam Hastings.

With Tommy during Jim's short spell as a player at Rugby Park.

■ 1965. When the brothers played table football it was competitive table football!

■ Willie doesn't think Dundee FC saw the best of Jim as a player, despite the intentions of John Prentice to make him the fulcrum of the team.

Dundee FC fan had to apologise

FAN TRIBUTE: IAIN DUNBAR.

I'VE been a United fan since 1978, when I was six years old. Although I didn't get to the League Cup win of '79, I saw them win our other four trophies.

When I was at Craigie High School in 1989, United trained opposite the school, on the pitch at the College of Education. A member of my class, a Dundee FC fan, shouted that United were "sh***".

Jim raced across to have a go at us. The boy who shouted that nonsense had to write a letter of apology to Jim, much to we United supporters' amusement!

Then, when we were relegated in '95, I sent Jim a letter on various things like new signings and season tickets for students.

His secretary replied and I was asked to meet Jim at the reception area of Tannadice to discuss the issues I'd raised. We spent about 20 minutes going through and explaining things, but he was great. I had been incredibly nervous before the meeting!

United training in the snow at Monymusk Park, February 1978.

■ August 1971. Jerry Kerr's last pre-season squad. Back, from left: Jim Cameron, Tommy Traynor, George Whisker, Donald Mackay, Hamish McAlpine, Walter Smith, Joe White, Morris Stevenson.

Middle: Jerry Kerr (manager), Joe Watson, Frank Esposito, Denis Gillespie, Sandy White, Alan Gordon, Campbell, Alec Reid, Rice, Billy Gray, Andy Dickson (physio), Doug Cowie (coach).

Front: Andy Rolland, Wilson Wood, Kenny Cameron, Ian Reid, Doug Smith, Alan Devlin, Davie Wilson, Stuart Markland, Jim Henry.

■ **July 1972. Jim' McLean's first pre-season squad. Back, from left: Frank Kopel, Sandy Davie, Hamish McAlpine, George Fleming.**

Middle: Jim McLean (manager), Jim Cameron, Jackie Copland, Walter Smith, Archie Knox, Pat Gardner, Tommy Traynor, Billy Gray, Andy Dickson (physiotherapist).

Front: Andy Rolland, Jim Henry, Joe Fascione, Sandy White, Doug Smith, Kenny Cameron, Ian Mitchell, Stuart Markland.

Jim was lapping Formula One Ferraris in a Morris Minor

TRIBUTE: CHICK YOUNG, RADIO AND TV PERSONALITY.

THERE was never much of a requirement to blow the bugle and put up the bunting at Tannadice in the days before his coming.

Dundee United had briefly nodded to and glimpsed at moments in the sun, but when wee Jim came, the Messiah walked in.

Jim McLean came from the grumpiest football family I have ever known.

Wee brother Tommy was a prince of moaners but Jim was the king.

By comparison the third man, Willie, was a diplomat but he too was capable of flirting with the family trait.

But they knew their game all right. Too true they did.

When I started in this business of football writing – and more than half a century has come and gone since I first walked into a newspaper office – it was a different world.

Different attitudes, different approaches, different relationships, and different access.

Eventually I was given the job of phoning on a daily basis the direct line of Jock Stein, Willie Waddell and Eddie Turnbull. It was a fine cure for the constipated. The young lad who fed the lions at the zoo or the army private on his first bomb disposal mission will understand the movements in my gut.

I used to stare at the phone like Scott Brown in the tunnel, searching for the mental strength and getting myself into the zone.

Sometimes it was a relief when they didn't answer. Your conscience told you that at least you had tried.

Mostly these giants of the game were gentle with a young reporter but there were days when you were swatted like a fly. I got to feel like a squash ball must.

But it was an apprenticeship for days still to come.

So when Wee Jum rocked up at United to succeed Jerry Kerr, who always struck me as being like your favourite grandpa, I took little notice.

He was a ridiculously young appointment and had been no more than a talented but workaday player.

At the tender age of 34 he toddled the journey from the neighbours at Dens, a trip so short that despite it being the Tayside mid-winter of '71-72 he would have gotten away without wearing a coat.

Which was handy because he rolled his sleeves up sharpish and piled into the job.

By 1974 Dundee United were in a cup final and James Yuille McLean's number was in my contacts book. Another gorilla in the jungle. He could go off on one, the touch paper ignited easily.

What he began to achieve at Dundee United was remarkable, like crossing the Atlantic on a paddle board. But it was his personality which engaged him so much with the gentlemen of the Fourth Estate. And I'm not being sexist. There were no women reporters around. Although I do concede you would have a right to question the "gentlemen" bit.

McLean struck as much fear at times into reporters as he did his players, who have taken a long time to reveal his legendary rants.

They weren't so brave telling tales out of school when the man was in his pomp.

He brought new rules to dealing with journalists. He banned – on and off, I think – my dear and sadly missed friend Dick Donnelly from Tannadice. A thumping punishment when you are a freelance in a two-horse town.

And they had been great muckers.

So maybe the distance softened whatever relationship I had with Jim.

I got on all right with him, and more importantly him with me. He maybe thought I wasn't in the west coast

April 6th, 1973. Jim visits the SFA offices in Glasgow. Not for the first time. Or the last time.

mafia, because I was there at Dens in 1983 when he won the title.

As representative of the Glasgow Evening Times I acknowledged my city's football royalty being dethroned by the upstarts from the east . . . while noting that the miracle-working managers of United and Aberdeen were west coast men.

Seems churlish to even bring it up, of course.

But his achievements were ridiculous. A European Cup semi-final, a UEFA cup final.

He was lapping Formula One Ferraris in a Morris Minor.

By the time the early nineties came in, the winds and tides of good fortune had swept me into a television career. One day I will try to understand how that happened.

But in Jim's last days as manager I persuaded him to sit down with me in the Tannadice boardroom and reflect on it all.

I went shopping for fireworks and came back with dynamite.

He opened up like I had never seen him do. It was as if the camera wasn't there and he was on a psychiatrist's couch.

It all rolled out about regretting not spending enough time with his family – an issue with which he desperately wanted to rewrite history – his love and admiration for Doris and a host of subjects which had forever been no-go areas.

And he smiled an impish, engaging smile which maybe was a collector's item that erased the classic image.

It was an astonishing piece of television which would have justified the whole programme, but we had to settle for maybe just half of it.

He bared his soul that day. He could have been manager of Rangers before Jock Wallace returned. And there were plenty other offers from elsewhere.

But he stuck with United and only strayed when big Jock Stein took him away with Scotland. If you ever want to see what a sorcerer and his apprentice look like, I refer you to those two.

We will never again see the likes of the wee man breathing fire on the touchline and standing, colossus-like, over a club.

For a while he was omnipotent at United, making players sign contracts which lasted longer than coastal erosion. Different times for sure.

But he was a tactical genius who knew a player when he saw one and who has a first-class honours degree in over-achievement.

It was a miracle.

I'd loved to have seen what he could have achieved with five loaves and a couple of fishes.

■ **August 2nd, 1997. Jim receives a 60th birthday cake from Chick before the first home league game of the '97-98 season.**

Happy 60th Birthday
Jim

The most honest man I ever met

FAN TRIBUTE: PETER CLARK.

IN 1999 I wrote a letter to Dundee United detailing my regrets about players like Steven Pressley and Erik Pedersen leaving, a lack of new signings, and my concerns about United's future.

I was 18, a season ticket holder and passionate about my club. A week later I was at work when my brother called me to say "a Jim McLean" had phoned the house asking to talk to me!

I immediately called Tannadice, spoke to a receptionist and said I was returning Jim McLean's call. She told me to hold on then Jim came on the phone.

He said he'd read my letter and invited me in to talk it over. I asked if it was OK to bring my dad with me (Jim had a fearsome reputation!)

My dad and I arranged to see Jim before the Rangers match that Saturday at Tannadice.

We arrived at reception and were told to go on up the stairs. Jim was at the top watching us . . . which set fear into me!

Jim and Derek Robertson sat us down in his office and within the first 10 minutes Jim had verbally destroyed my letter. The meeting lasted half an hour, during which we talked about various issues related to United – in colourful language! He was up-front and entirely honest, pulling sheets of paper from his desk which detailed the contracts and money he'd offered players to stay and spoke about the situation surrounding a possible merger with Dundee.

He thanked me for coming to meet him, offered me tickets for the match (but we had season tickets) and also said to help myself to the buffet in the boardroom.

This was Jim McLean, the most honest man I ever met. I will always remember that day.

FAN TRIBUTE: RONNIE MOLLISON.

I'VE been a United fan all my life. A memory that always stayed with me is from when I was maybe nine or 10.

I was in town with my mum and decided to wait in Castle Street while she went into a shop. It was a winter afternoon and I was wearing my United scarf.

The passenger window of an Audi car I was close to went down and the driver said, "So you're a United fan?" I looked in the car and it was Jim McLean.

We chatted briefly before he reached over and gave me a handful of United postcards with the team and their signatures on. I was over the moon and couldn't wait to tell my mum all about it. All because he saw a laddie standing there with a scarf on.

■ In the Dens Park dressing room after the 1979 League Cup win. Those were great days.

Tactics and standards of behaviour

PLAYER TRIBUTE: ALLAN PRESTON.

ALLAN PRESTON, now a respected radio pundit, pays Jim a really quite remarkable tribute, which goes beyond the world of football. In Allan's words:

Everything I have become in my life, everything I've achieved, is, I believe, because I have self-discipline. This was instilled in me by my parents, of course, but also in my professional life by the standards of behaviour Jim McLean demanded of me, and all the apprentices at Tannadice.

I started training with United when I was 11 years old, signing S-forms at 12. United's Edinburgh signings trained on a blaes pitch at what is now the Institute of Sport. The Aberdeen kids trained on a Wednesday night, Glasgow was Thursday nights, but we were Tuesdays. Jim McLean, with Wattie Smith, Kenny Cameron, Jimmy Bone, Gordon Wallace, whoever was his assistant at the time, would attend all of those sessions.

And it was good training.

We would be taught to control the ball across our bodies on the move, take a touch with your left foot that put the ball in the ideal place to make a pass with your right (or vice-versa), making sure to get our heads up at the same time to judge exactly where we were putting the ball.

Then deliver a pass to a striker's "safe side" where he could shield it from a defender.

Jim's training was basically the same for kids as for the first team. We were being prepared to slot in to a method of playing that would make us instantly useful, instantly able to understand team orders. It's the way Barcelona's La Masia academy does things nowadays. Jim was doing it 50 years ago.

He would tell us that the foundation of the team was the back four, and that this base had to stay solid at all times. If one full-back went forward, then the other would sit in. We had a proper shape at all times, everyone knew their job.

As a wide man, Jim would tell me that a confident winger goes past his man on the outside. A winger cutting inside is looking for help.

And he would test you mentally to strengthen you for the tough things that lay ahead. He'd take you into the office on a Friday and tell you that you were playing for the first team the next day. He'd prepare you for it, but also watch to see how you reacted. It was all designed to test your character.

The discipline was rigid. Every one of the young players had a job.

Mine was to wash the kit, get everything in an industrial washing machine, then dried in a giant tumble drier. One Friday when I was 16, I got all the first team kit, except Maurice Malpas's socks. He still had them on, getting treatment from the physios. I washed and dried the rest of the kit, then got Mo's socks. I put them in the washing machine on their own and left them, thinking I'd get them dried first thing Monday morning, no harm done.

I got a phone call from Jim at my parents' house in Edinburgh that night, asking why there was a pair of socks not dried?

He made me come up to Dundee, on the 6am train the next morning, to dry those socks.

I didn't like it much at the time but it taught me a vitally important life lesson – never leave a job unfinished. And that has stayed with me all my life. I do everything the best I can possibly do it. Every time.

I have Jim to thank for that.

But if some of his ideas were old fashioned, he was years ahead of his time in lots of other ways.

We had everything at Tannadice. All the stuff they call sports science nowadays, Jim was doing 40 years ago. We had sessions with psychiatrists to strengthen us mentally, we had Stuart Hogg as a sprint coach, we had nutritionists telling us what to eat and when to eat it.

And Jim told you how you played. Really told you.

After every game, whether first team, under-age teams or reserves, he'd go round the team from goalkeeper to the strikers telling us exactly how we'd performed. Plusses and negatives. It was the truth.

He'd warn us that when we went out of the dressing room, families and friends would always say we'd had a good game, and if that is said enough then you'll begin to believe, "I wasn't too bad, then". He said he and his coaches would always give it to us straight. Good game,

Allan as he was when breaking into United's first team.

bad game, and point out things that had to improve. He was always trying to improve us, so to make an improvement you have to know what the flaw is. It was an idea I took into my later career.

When I became assistant-manager at Macclesfield, I phoned Alex Ferguson asking if I could come in and observe their training and man-management techniques at Manchester United.

Fergie took me along, but all he wanted to talk about was Jim. How he was years ahead of his time, the most incredible professional, and all the things Jim did that were very good practice.

He told me a great story, though.

Jim was a friend, but also a rival of Fergie's. One Sunday night at 11pm Jim phoned Fergie's house to accuse him of "tapping" Paul Sturrock. Fergie utterly denied it, he hadn't done it. Jim said, "Well somebody has then". Fergie always wondered if Jim went on to phone every other manager in Scotland that night, accusing each of them. He probably did.

The day after the 1991 Cup Final, we kids were playing in the final of a tournament in Holland.

Despite what had gone on the previous day, all the stuff that was attached to a Scottish Cup Final, and one that is often cited as the best of all time, Jim and Walter Smith flew out in the early hours of the Sunday morning to watch our game. And we won. We had to win!

He always did his job the best he could.

I signed one of the famous eight-year contracts, of course. Four years, with a four-year option. The pay wasn't great, but the win bonuses were amazing. Jim would reward success and did everything he could to make us successful.

One time, a Tuesday, the hard running day if we didn't have a midweek game, he brought out a bag of balls. "Great", we thought. "We're getting a game". Jim ran us until we were half-dead, until our lungs were turning inside out . . . then put the balls away. He'd driven us to run as hard as we possibly could, with the prize of a game if we did well. He'd got the very best physical effort out of us.

And I remember the 36-stage circuit training stints Andy Dickson did. It would demolish us! But I remember how well the older pros coped with it. Jim was training us up to be super-fit athletes.

Once you got used to it, the demands it made of your body, the benefits were there for all to see. No team ever ran us off the park. Never came up against a team fitter than us. If you had a man to mark, or a slot you had to fill, then even if you'd just made a lung-bursting 60-yard run, you had to be back in position right away. Being tired wasn't an acceptable excuse.

The changing room was great too, brilliant lads.

Jim was a hard man with us, an incredibly disciplined person himself, who demanded discipline from his team. He was a football genius. A brilliant man. I learned an enormous amount about the game and how to play it.

But also lessons about life, responsibilities and personal standards of behaviour that have stuck with me to this day.

I'll always be grateful to Jim McLean, for football and personal reasons.

■ **Allan in the Dundee United under-16s team that went to Northern Ireland and won the Milk Cup, beating Newcastle United's u-16s 4-0 in the final, in 1986. Back, from left: Paddy Connolly, John Bishop, Mike McAdams, Shaun McSkimming, Martin Feenie, Alec Cleland. Front: Scott Kopel, John McQuillan, Ray McKinnon, Allan Preston, J. McCreadie.**

■ Lorraine and Steve, a romance made at Tannadice!

A great man and an admirable woman

TRIBUTE: LORRAINE KELLY.

WHEN Dundee United had their terrific run in the UEFA and Scottish Cups in 1987 I was the Scottish correspondent for TVam and interviewed Jim on a weekly basis.

He called me his "lucky mascot". I reckon I was THE most biased sports reporter ever.

While everyone else seemed to be covering the Old Firm, I'd be setting up at Tannadice with my cameraman Steve, who would become my husband, and was also a lifelong United fan.

In fact, Steve and I had our first ever date when he asked me out to see United play at home against Hearts in 1985. I fell in love with the team and also, of course, with Steve.

Sadly, as we all know, United were runners up in two competitions in 1987. It was very hard to bear, but still a brilliant experience.

I remember Jim used to always greet me with a big smile, which to be honest, unnerved everyone at the club. I think they were more used to a frown, but he was always so very kind to me. At that time there were very few women who covered football, and his seal of approval meant so much.

Of course behind every successful man there is a supportive and understanding woman, and I don't think Jim would have been anywhere near as successful without his wonderful wife Doris. She really is the unsung heroine of this story. Doris never complained when Jim came home fuming after a defeat.

She was his rock and I am in complete awe of the way she has taken care of him since he became ill, with such patience and kindness.

■ **Lorraine's TVam days.**

Jim was old school. He could be difficult, tough and chippy, but he had such passion for the game and he cared so deeply about Dundee United.

We will never see his like again and he will always be one of my favourite interviewees, just as Doris will always be one of the people I most admire.

Fitter than dogs

FAN TRIBUTE: GRANT MILLAR.

PERHAPS like many United fans of a certain age, I've briefly encountered Jim McLean in person at various stages in my life.

The first time I "met" him was Monifieth Beach in the summer of 1974, when United were doing pre-season training on the long-lost dunes.

While the players were taking a break, my star-struck nine-year-old self wandered among them to gather autographs before venturing to ask for Mr McLean's autograph, which he kindly gave.

It never occurred to me that they were at work and not to be disturbed – they were all friendly and polite. My abiding memory from the day is of the whippet-like Graeme Payne winning all the sprints (regardless of whether there were hurdles or not), and how they all looked much fitter than any butcher's dog I'd ever seen.

Then up at Tannadice over the seasons, I'd see Jim in and out of the dug-out.

As the years passed and Jim and Tannadice changed, I'd see him sitting, white-shirted and grey-trousered, in his personal executive box behind the dug-out. But when it was required (or allowed – touchline bans being commonplace back then), I often smiled as he suddenly appeared like a Jack-in-a-box and raced down the stairs to the dug-out, and then back up again once some hapless

3
17
2

soul had been "well telt". Quite right, too, and as much part of the Tannadice entertainment bonus as a pie-eating contest or trying to decipher the equations on the half-time scoreboard.

Our next interaction was in the early '80s. United were at home to St Mirren, but there was torrential rain. So I phoned Tannadice to ask if the game was on. I don't think I was the only one phoning, as the line seemed permanently engaged.

Eventually I got through and was greeted with an instantly recognisable "Yes?" Oh, it's himself, I realised. "Is the game on?" I asked. "Game's on", Jim replied succinctly and put the phone down before I could say "Okay, thanks". But I remember being impressed that he answered the phone himself – always the sign of a conscientious worker.

The ref postponed the game about ten minutes before kick-off, I recall, but that wasn't Jim's fault.

In 1983, in the week after United won the league, I played in a juveniles cup final in Arbroath and Jim came down to present the trophy. True to the final hurdle form of that time, the Dundee team lost the final. But it was an evening match and Jim turned out to watch the game and stayed to present the trophy. It shows that he was generous (maybe too generous?) with his spare time, and at a very busy period for him, too.

Then in 1987, I went to Gothenburg for the first leg of the UEFA Cup Final. On the day of the game, there was a "friendly" between United staff and various Scottish journalists and media people.

A friend and I somehow ended up watching this game of "jaiket goalposts fitba", and we took photos at the game. I didn't meet Jim that time, but it was a different setting from usual and a svelte-looking Jim seemed to be fair enjoying himself at this relatively light-hearted kickabout.

Still in 1987, I used to get the bus along Arbroath Road and sometimes saw Jim jogging from the Northern College playing fields (where United used to train) back to Tannadice. He must have been on a fitness drive at the time – too much ice cream was the problem, I recall.

Given the adversarial nature of the football rivalry in Dundee, I remember thinking, "Oh Jim, you're brave!"

In the late '80s, I worked as a postie for a while and sometimes delivered letters to the McLean home in Broughty Ferry. He was always very polite whenever I met him.

Slightly later, a friend started videoing United's home matches for Jim and I sometimes helped him lug the equipment up to the TV gantry in "The Gods" section of the main stand. After the game, we stored the equipment in Jim's office, so I said "Hello" to Jim on a few occasions when visiting his office.

I'm sure there are many Arabs with similar mini-tales of encountering Jim, tales which perhaps help to shed light on his character.

Indeed, the very fact that there will be many United fans who could list their various encounters with him, shows how Jim McLean was – still is, and always will be – one of Dundee's great characters, and part of the city's landscape (once the statue is unveiled) and also our memoryscape.

Jim at the "jaikets for goalposts" match v. the Press corps in Gothenburg.

Jim told me: 'You'll have to change'

PLAYER TRIBUTE: PAUL STURROCK.

IF Jim McLean can be described as a unique figure in the history of Scottish football so, too, can his relationship with one of his greatest players at Dundee United.

The man in question is Paul Sturrock, who spent his entire playing career under the great man before going on to coach and then manage the Tangerines under him.

And after a successful career as a manager on both sides of the Border with clubs like St Johnstone, Plymouth Argyle and Sheffield Wednesday, "Luggy" admits no other single figure influenced his time in the game more than Jim McLean.

Signed on an S-form in the early seventies, he would play almost 400 games for Jim's United, then spend five years coaching under him before finally managing the team for just under two years from 1998.

Through each of these periods, Paul is in no doubt about the vast knowledge he picked up from the man it's fair to call his mentor.

"If I start at the beginning, he played a massive part in making me the player I was," Paul says. "As an amateur and early on at United, my pace meant I was a striker who ran beyond defences. It served me well and got me goals, but after a while Jim came to me and told me I had to change.

"He said fast as I was, teams were becoming wise to me and if I didn't add more to my game, my career would stall. So, for about five years I did extra work with Wattie Smith and Gordon Wallace that focused on me taking the ball into feet and linking.

"Jim also insisted I learn to play on the wing as well as through the middle, and it made my career. It meant I could still run in behind, but also come short for the ball to link the play, or move out wide. It kept teams guessing as to what I was going to do and it's why I achieved what I did as a player."

By the time the boots were hung up in 1989, Paul was already part of the coaching staff at Tannadice and over the next five seasons he believes he got an unrivalled education on that side of the game.

"It was tough and at times I was getting back at seven in the morning from watching players down in England and going straight to training, but that was the kind of energy Jim had and he expected the same from others.

"He would hardly miss a game or training session, from the S-forms right up to the first team. And if he wasn't somewhere at a game at night he'd be reading about football or watching games from all over the world.

"Back when most people didn't have it, he had a massive satellite TV system that he could adjust to pick up games from places like Brazil and Uruguay, as well as all over Europe, so he was always studying the game.

"Likewise, when it came to our training, I had to take notes on every session. It became like my Bible and we knew what worked and what didn't and when the team or individuals should be working on certain things. He was always big on that and hammered into me that football was about the team, but also the individual."

After heading down the A90 to earn his managerial spurs at the Perth Saints, Paul returned to United as team boss in September 1998 and witnessed Jim McLean as club chairman, a role that often seemed to have him at war with himself.

"Jim was a genius as a manager and like all managers everything was about making the team better. As chairman, though, he also had to try to balance the books.

"I remember us going into the winter break third in the league and then Rangers came in for Billy Dodds, who was having a great season. I obviously didn't want to sell him, and as a manager himself Jim knew how I felt, but in the end he believed he had that duty to balance the books, so Billy was sold and we ended up finishing eighth.

"As chairman I think he struggled with things like that. He also had a thing about being accused of interfering because I'd been a player under him.

"The irony was throughout my career elsewhere he would always keep in touch and tell me what he thought about my teams. He'd phone at all times of the day and even send me letters going through the team's strengths and weaknesses.

"I didn't always agree with him, but I always welcomed his input. To have someone with his knowledge of the game giving me advice was never a bad thing in my eyes. It just became more awkward for him when I was managing United."

An ordinary Scottish family, that just happens to be quite extraordinary

FAMILY TRIBUTE: DORIS MCLEAN.

DORIS McLEAN appears to be a typical Scottish lady, of the sort that once made Scots a people who carried politeness and respectability in their DNA. Because no one would want reports of loutish behaviour to reach their mother.

She is dignified and slightly reserved, sizing up a stranger like me to see what sort of person I am before deciding whether she will talk to me.

She hasn't been too well recently, she explains at the door of her beautiful home, and so hasn't been paying the best of attention to her housework. Whatever she means by this isn't readily apparent. Her home is spotless.

It takes only a few minutes to discern that she is a canny, clever woman. And fiercely proud of her husband and family.

We chat. The weather, the city of Dundee, my family, the project I'm doing. She is a lovely woman, entirely without airs or graces.

Once her trust is gained (the sign of acceptance is her offering me a cup of tea) she is warm and friendly. Most of all, now we have a cuppa in our hands, she is very open.

We talk about her trip to see Phil Differ's play, *Smile*. She had been concerned about it. The early script she was shown had too many swear words for her liking. But the play had won her seal of approval. She had enjoyed it and thought that it captured her husband well.

Doris isn't really an everyday Scottish housewife, of course. She is married to a quite remarkable man.

She smiles as she recalls the late-1950s evening when she was 18 and a joiner named James ask her to dance at Hamilton Trocadero Dance Hall.

Doris was from Airdrie and worked in the office of a clothing firm.

The young man wasn't only a joiner, he also played football part-time. And dancing wouldn't be a thing he did an awful lot of. "He never liked it," she chuckles. "Whenever we went to a dinner-dance or a function I was well warned: 'one dance' he'd say. He never liked dancing."

James and Doris "clicked", as folk used to say, and started dating right away, then were married in 1961.

Doris allowed this photo, from her wedding album, to be used.

Doris and Jim were married in 1961.

Doris got used to living with a football man. Except, firstly, Jim wasn't a footballer at that time. He was a joiner.

All through his career with Hamilton Accies and Clyde, Jim worked on building sites during the day, while training in the evenings and playing on Saturdays. It wasn't until he was transferred to Dundee, at the age of 28, in 1965, that he became a full-time footballer.

He kept his hand in, though. He built three homes, of successively larger sizes, during his time in the city of Dundee.

Each time doing the joinery work (and much more) himself. The last home, however, was one that he and Doris bought. It had always been a house that Doris

NEWS PROFILE

DUNDEE UNITED'S manager Jim McLean, one of the most successful ever in his profession, is at the centre of the European football stage this week as his team prepares to take on IFK Gothenburg in the first leg of the UEFA Cup final. His wife Doris, however, has deliberately kept out of the spotlight. Here, in an exclusive and extremely rare interview, a "Courier" reporter takes a look—

Inside the very private world of Mrs Jim McLean

Mrs McLean relaxing at home before the most exciting period in United's history

66 *Football is first and foremost it's his job, and it's our security and what's good for him is good for us* **99**

66 *With the European games coming so close together, it seems I've just unpacked one suitcase when I'm packing another.* **99**

■ Doris gave The Courier a rare interview in the run-up to the UEFA Cup Final in 1987.

■ Right, This is the photo that was used.

had admired from afar and she was very pleased to get it when it came up for sale.

So, apart from joinery, what did this most football-oriented of men enjoy away from the game?

"He has always liked cowboy films," laughs Doris, amused by my mundane questions about Jim's personal likes. "When he wasn't watching football on TV he liked Frank Sinatra, Neil Diamond and Kenny Rogers. He found Morecambe & Wise really funny. They were his favourites.

"Food? He likes plain stuff, steak and egg with chips. But he'd always look at the dessert menu first when we went out. He had a sweet tooth. Though he wouldn't go out at all if the team lost."

She is even more amused when I ask if she likes football. "No," she says, smiling. She indicates the room we are in and says, "Jim would watch football in here, I'd be through there, watching my soaps.

"I went to home games, but mostly worked in the

Left: The family's photograph of Jim being awarded an Honorary Doctorate in Law from the University of Dundee, in 2011.

Right: The 1991 Scottish Cup Final is known throughout Scottish football as the "family final". For Doris, that really is her family. Her husband Jim and brother-in-law Tom are pictured leading out their teams. Poignantly, the final was staged just a few days after their father, also named Tom, had died.

32

office with Ella (club secretary Mrs Lindsay) counting the programmes money. But I watched the big games, and I'd sometimes go to watch Jim, back when he was playing."

She then tells a story that surprises, although also doesn't surprise me.

For every game, the Tannadice boardroom was used to greet and entertain the visiting directors and dignitaries. Doris made it her job to furnish the place with fresh flowers each time. This was fine with Jim – but he made her pay for the flowers herself. This wasn't to be an expense set against the club.

I ask Doris about Jim's early management career. We talk of his move from being a coach at Dundee FC to take over from Jerry Kerr as manager of United.

"He would have stayed at Dens, he was enjoying working with the players there. He was getting his ideas across to them and they seemed to be enjoying it too. But he didn't agree with the way the Gellatlys (the family who were then the Dundee directors) ran the club."

Doris's tone of voice reveals her feelings on the matter. If the Gellatly father and son dynasty at Dens Park were against her husband, then she has but the lowest of regard for them.

She brightens when speaking of John Prentice, who had been manager of Dundee and the man who persuaded Jim to return to Dens from Kilmarnock and try football coaching. Doris had liked Mr Prentice.

"He and Jim loved to talk football. They agreed on a lot. He liked and admired Jock Stein, too, they got on very well together. And Bobby Seith (a member of Dundee FC's 1962 championship-winning side, who went on to be manager of Preston and Hearts). Bobby knew football, Jim would say, he wanted his teams to play the game properly."

But her tone hardens a little when talking of Jim's first few months at Tannadice. "Once he was over the road, Jim had to tell Jerry Kerr not to interfere," she says. "He was still there behind the scenes, he was general manager. Jim would say that if he was to do the job, then he'd do it in his own way. But he really liked and respected Johnston Grant, the chairman at Tannadice. He was a fine man, a gentleman."

What was Jim like as a family man?

Doris's openness is even more apparent. "Jim would tell you he'd been a disgrace as a father," she reveals. "He used to say he was away far too much. He'd say that he had spent more time with his players than his sons. Jim would be home for his tea at 4.30pm, then out again by five because he'd go to watch the S-signings training, or when the club had the Jim McLean Training School at Gussie Park he felt that he had to be fully involved in that because it was something that had his name on it."

Doris has decided she trusts me enough to let me

■ Jim working on son Colin's back-post crossing technique in the mid-60s, although Colin never really was infected by the football bug.

see her family collection of photos. She agrees to allow some to be used in this book. She even lets me use a photo from her wedding album, which means I must take the entire album away to scan. This is a sign of trust, but it terrifies me. What if I crash my car? What if I somehow lose Jim McLean's wedding album?

We look at the proclamation, an impressive document, granting Jim the Freedom of the City of Dundee, which is framed on the wall. It is clearly a distinction she is proud of, recognition given by the city fathers.

"Jim is proud of this too," she says. "It was a thing from the city, not just a football thing."

Another photo, showing Jim being awarded an honorary doctorate of law, by Dundee University, is a matter of equal pride. She allows me to take away both of these personal artefacts. I'm even more nervous.

I feel we now know each other well enough to ask a more personal question. What was Jim's personality away from the game?

Doris thinks before answering.

Talking of private matters doesn't come easily to Scottish people and, in truth, it is an odd question. How often is anyone asked to list the personal traits of their spouse for publication? And, unlike most people, there is the added strangeness of there having been thousands of newspaper column inches written about Jim McLean over the years.

But a lot of it was nonsense-talk about a man that Doris wouldn't recognise. "These people didn't really know him", she says.

This is where her strength of character shines through. She talks of her relationship with her husband. "I'd always back him. No matter what, I'd always back him. I went to every home game.

"If he had gone to Rangers when he was offered that job, I'd have fully supported him in doing that. We talked about it and I told him to do what he felt was right. He didn't go because it would have meant upsetting the boys and making us move home. Quite a few other clubs offered him jobs. Newcastle, for instance. But he didn't fancy it. We were happy here."

Doris tells me one thing that brings a lump to my throat, though it is, on the face of it, an innocuous few words. She says, "He always got up in the morning and every day he worked really hard."

That sentence doesn't look like much. You have to understand the depth of mid-20th Century Scottish values to fully "get" what she means by this. Jim provided for his family. He did the very best he could at every thing he did, every day. Absolutely every single thing. And this is a matter of pride to her.

I'm going to leave that thought with you. Because if you understand, then you understand. If you don't, you probably never will. Scottish working-class values are a thing you have to have lived. Jim understood that.

Doris continues, and reveals what perhaps might be a surprise. "Most of all, Jim is by nature a very shy man," she says. "Not at football, mind, not in the dug-out. He

Jim, Doris and family in the mid-1960s.

always had very clear ideas on what he thought about football.

"But he wouldn't like to stand up and do an after-dinner speech. He'd happily do question-and-answer sessions, and say what he thought, but not public speaking. And he wouldn't ever push himself forward in a crowd, he'd sit in the corner and be quiet."

She looks me in the eye, having decided that if she is to sum up her husband in a few words, then this is it. "He is honest," she says. "He is always completely honest. He'll say what he thinks, no matter what. Whether good or bad, he never, ever lied to you. You always knew where you were with him."

■ **Doris kept a few of the football cards that used to be so popular in Scotland.**

She's right. Everyone always knew where they were with Jim.

Any of you reading this, I can promise you'd like and admire Doris McLean. She is, in the same way she describes her beloved husband, entirely honest. No one could fail to take to her because she is a generous, genuinely nice, down-to-earth person. She is a trusting person.

Jim was very fortunate when he chose to tap this particular pretty girl on the shoulder, that far-off night at Hamilton Trocadero.

FAMILY TRIBUTE: COLIN AND GARY McLEAN.

A WEEK after my visits to speak to Doris, I was back at Jim McLean's house to interview his sons, Colin and Gary. They rarely give interviews of any nature and I consider it a coup that they agreed to talk to me about their father.

Mind you, I'd defy any United supporter to approach

■ **Every schoolboy's dream! Gary with the League Cup in 1979.**

a meeting with a McLean man and not wonder: "Are they like their dad?"

And they are. In their different ways, and to different degrees. But yes, you can see Jim in both of them. Neither suffers fools gladly but would express this in different ways.

Gary, the younger brother by six years, would tell you straight out if he didn't like what you were saying. Colin, who physically looks more like Jim, is the more reserved of the two, and just wouldn't give you the time of day if he took agin you.

They both have a down-to-earth attitude about what it was like to be raised by a man who is the subject of so many stories, so many opinions, and exists in such high regard for so many people.

My first two questions are obvious: do you like football, and (most importantly) are you United fans?

Both of them answer the second question first. They are United supporters at heart. Gary fully self-identifies as a fan, though doesn't go to Tannadice much these days.

Colin isn't much of a football man, which strikes me as surprising, as he must have been surrounded by it all of his life. But he says that yes, if pressed for an answer, United are his team.

The brothers exchange a few words between themselves on this, clarifying how each of them views the club. Gary accuses his brother (good-naturedly, but in tones only brothers can use

Family celebrations in the McLean household sometimes included silverware being delivered.

CHAMPIONS 198

with each other) of not going to see United enough to be termed a supporter.

"I am a supporter, though," Colin asserts. Doris chips in to say that, yes, they both like Dundee United.

There is a slight undercurrent to this and it takes me a little while to fully appreciate what the family mean. I have to re-run the way they say it in my memory to fully "get" what they are talking about.

It is a nuance of perspective. Ordinary fans like me regard United as something that is ours (all fans refer to football teams as "us": as in, "we played well today" or "we should never have lost that"). But in reality we punters aren't really so involved.

This is a much deeper thing for Jim McLean's sons. When they say they are United men, they are expressing support for their father, their family history, as well as the club he so memorably managed.

The concept of Dundee United runs in their blood because they, like all of us, for a long time regarded Dundee United as a part of Jim McLean as much as we thought of Jim McLean as part of Dundee United.

Pride in the tangerine, pride in the club for Colin and

■ **Having built quite a few homes for his family in Dundee, and a development of eight houses (with his brother Willie) when he played for Hamilton, Jim knew what he was talking about when it came to joinery work, or (as seen left) roofing and bricklaying. (Pic courtesy of Dave Martin, Fotopress.)**

■ Gary at Tannadice, doing joinery work for the club . . . with Jim in the background pointing out the tactical advantages of keeping your head up, looking for a through-ball between the centre-half and full-back, while sawing.

Gary is also pride in their father and they are, to a huge degree, proud of their father.

This is a theme I detected throughout all my dealings with the McLean family, even when talking to Jim's brother Willie. They are immensely proud of Jim and what he achieved. But no one ever actually says the words: "We are very proud of him", which is another very Scottish thing. We don't do that in this country, it sounds too much like boasting.

They don't have to say the words, though, it is obvious. When Colin says he is a Dundee United supporter, it is because it was his father's life and work and he supports and is proud of that. Gary, as you'll read below, tells me about how good it was to work with his father. They don't have to use words like "pride".

I ask what it was like to grow up sharing a Dundee United legend with all the supporters. "He was just our Dad," says Gary. "It was normal, it was our life," agrees Colin. "We didn't know any other way," rounds off Gary.

What do they think of Jim's reputation as an angry man. "It was mostly just paper talk," says Gary. "It was to sell newspapers. He wasn't like that. He had standards he expected, but he was very, very fair-minded."

The brothers, and Doris, talk about their reaction to Phil Differ's Dundee Rep play, *Smile* (see page 240). They had been wary of it because although they had read the script, as Gary points out these things can be slanted in different ways depending on where the actors and director want to take it. But all three are united in their assessment that it was an enjoyable, balanced thing.

Gary was a good player in his day and remembers, slightly ruefully, what Jim used to say to him when he watched Forthill United Under-12s. "He always forgot that I wasn't Paul Sturrock", says Gary.

"He'd tell me how I played and sometimes say that Sturrock wouldn't have done it that way. But not many people were Paul Sturrock."

Jim, probably unsurprisingly, would give his trademark honest assessment of football, whether it was his son playing or not.

But though he didn't become a professional footballer, Gary did work with his father and retains fond memories of doing so. "I spent a lot of time with him," he says. "On the one hand he was away a lot, but often I spent time with him either on away trips with United or at the ground.

"Dad and I had good, quality time together carrying out repairs and joinery work at Tannadice. He wouldn't have the club pay for things that he, or we, could do ourselves.

He kept me right as to what was needing done and would teach me how to do things. We'd talk about, and

■ Always a generous man when it came to charities, Jim bid for a "Guided tour of RAF Leuchars" in one of Radio Tay's Caring for Kids campaigns in the 80s. Colin went along too.

RESCUE
EXPLOSIVE

argue about, which type of joint would be best to use. We did it the best way, the way it would last longest, not the quickest way. It's something I've taken with me all through my life.

"I feel lucky to have spent so much time working with Dad, and also sharing a love of football with him.

"He is a perfectionist. If he does a job it has to be done right. This was true when he made or fixed things himself, or when he supervised me doing things.

"And it was the same when he had the players training, if they were doing 100 metre sprints then they sprinted until five metres past the finish line and didn't slow up before it.

"I learned a lot from him about doing things right, doing the best you can possibly do, every single job you take on."

Gary says this in a matter-of-fact way, but there is again a strong feeling of that unspoken pride.

This reminiscing leads to a touching, and amusing, moment between the family, a memory they all clearly find very funny.

They recount: "the Princess Grace incident".

In the UEFA Cup of 1981-82 (that campaign also included the famous 5-0 thrashing of Borussia Monchengladbach) United had drawn the most aristocratic club in Europe in the first round.

AS Monaco, financially backed by the Monegasque royal family, His Serene Highness Prince Rainier of Monaco (to give the laddie his full and proper title) and his wife, former Oscar-winning Hollywood superstar Grace Kelly.

Grace had designed the diagonally-halved strip that Monaco wore, replacing the red-and-white stripes they previously played in.

United, sadly lacking strips designed by a film star princess, went to the principality on the French south coast to play Les Rouge et Blancs and, in Dundee football parlance, "handed them their arse on a plate", winning 5-2.

The prince and princess, mesmerised by the incredible United performance, came to Tannadice for the return leg, on September 30th, 1981, clearly hoping to see more tangerine magic. But a poor United showing allowed Monaco to win 2-1 (although United still won the tie on aggregate).

Jim wasn't at all pleased with the United team's efforts at Tannadice. He felt the players had let the home fans down. In the dressing room after the final whistle he outlined his feelings to them in no uncertain terms, in detail, at length, and using language appropriate for Scottish football.

Waiting close by to be presented to Jim after the game were the prince and princess, who sat twiddling their thumbs, listening to Jim's assessment of the

■ Princess Grace of Monaco arriving at Tannadice in 1981.

failings of his midfield and the lack of penetrating runs made by the forwards.

The United staff offered the royals a cup of tea while they waited, though.

All families have funny moments from the past to share. Moments that are brought up often, and retain their humour even though the story has been told many times at get-togethers.

It's just that the McLean family's memories involve Jim McLean: legend.

They are a decent, down-to-earth, typical family. I came away from the interview with a feeling of admiration for Colin and Gary.

I liked them as people. They are good guys – who just happen to be the sons of Jim McLean: Dundee United Legend.

Imagine, if you will, what is must have been like to be the family of Jim McLean. He was as famous, in the Dundee area, as a film star. People would nudge each other when he and Doris walked into restaurants and say, "There's Jim McLean". Whenever Colin or Gary gave their names, they were identified as Jim's sons.

Those of us who merely look on from outside cannot possibly appreciate what that was like. Film stars and royalty get police protection squads and in-depth media training to deal with this sort of stuff.

Doris, Colin and Gary just got on with it.

Jim and Doris with their "other" family at the 1981 DUFC end-of-season dinner-dance.

What a shower!

FAN TRIBUTE: KEVIN REID, EX-KIRKTON, NOW CUMBRIA.

I TRAVELLED with the team to the famous 5-2 away win against AS Monaco.

On boarding the plane for the flight home I was reading the match report in *Nice Matin* (a French newspaper) when I felt a tap on my shoulder. I turned to find the great man beside me. "What are the papers saying?" he asked.

I told him the headline was *La Douche Ecossaise* and that its literal meaning was: The Scottish Shower.

Before I could say anything else he set off on an unrepeatable rant against the French Press!

When he paused for breath I added that it had a figurative meaning, summing up how United's performance on the night came as a great shock to the hosts.

He looked me straight in the eye and said, "How did you no' say that in the first place then!" before turning round and heading back to his seat.

In that moment I got a wee insight into how some of the players must have felt at times! Looking back, I guess it must have been like walking on eggshells around him. As they say, though, you have to break a few eggs to make an omelette!

What he achieved was remarkable. Legend of a man!

■ **United back from Monaco, September 17th, 1981.**

16
STAND
SECTION C
ADULTS £2·50P
JUVENILES £1·20P
ALL JUVENILES MUST BE PAID FOR

Jim always kept in touch with Ray

PLAYER TRIBUTE: RAY McKINNON.

BY the time his Dundee United side were regularly challenging for trophies towards the end of the 1970s, Jim McLean had earned a deserved reputation for producing excellent home-grown talent.

When the end of his managerial reign came in the summer of 1993, the Tangerines' youth policy and the conveyor belt of fine players it had produced was the envy of clubs around the country.

As has been highlighted elsewhere in this book, some of those who emerged through the ranks at Tannadice were of the highest quality. Men who went on to perform at the top level in club and international football.

Names like Andy Gray, Raymond Stewart, Paul Sturrock, Dave Narey and Maurice Malpas will always spring to mind quickly when the subject of United's youth policy in raised, but it was not just at that elite level the work Jim and his scouting staff excelled.

Down the years, literally hundreds of players who would go on to have solid careers were produced and there can be barely a Scottish club that has not benefited from the contribution of a performer whose early days were spent at Tannadice.

Even now, the best part of three decades since Jim departed as manager, his influence on our game remains apparent.

Former United kids like Ray McKinnon and Gary Bollan are still plying their trade as managers on the Scottish club scene, while through his work with the BBC, another Tannadice product, Allan Preston, is currently one of the country's most respected media pundits having, we shouldn't forget, also spent a decent few years in coaching and management.

Whether their time working as players under him was short or long, it's fair to say most, if not all, of those on the list of graduates from the Tannadice youth academy have taken at least some of what they learned under Jim McLean into their management years and put it to good use.

That's certainly the case for one of those old boys, Ray McKinnon.

Ray would go on and manage United for a spell and is currently in charge at newly-turned-professional Queen's Park.

"The big thing I took into management and that I learned from Jim is that every day, however far away the next game is, standards have to be high," he says.

"I would say I am more relaxed in training than Jim was and I like to have a good time and a laugh.

"If the players are not right at it, though, we stop and start over again and that's definitely something I got from him.

"He demanded the highest of standards all the time

and I even remember in my second spell as a player at United when his brother Tommy was gaffer and Jim was chairman, he walked past training one day and as soon as he appeared the intensity went up a level."

As his career at United was kicking off, midfielder Ray also quickly learned that, as fearsome as Jim could be at times, he did listen to his players, even if he seldom acknowledged doing so.

"Just after I broke into the first team as a teenager he blasted me at half-time in a game because I wasn't getting on the ball enough.

"I answered him back and said the first-half had been like a game of tennis with the ball going from one end to another and all I was doing was chasing it up and down the park.

"He had a real go at me for talking back, but come the next game his team talk was all about retaining possession and making sure we got the midfield into the game.

"That was Jim, he might not give you credit at the time, but he would think about what you'd said and if he thought you were right, he'd act."

With both men not being afraid to express their opinions, Ray's time under Jim included a couple of well-publicised bust-ups, but Ray is happy to set the record straight about their relationship.

"I think people thought we didn't get on, but we actually did and I always had huge respect for him. After he sold me to Nottingham Forest he would phone me almost every Friday to see how I was doing.

Ray at the time of his United first-team debut.

"That mattered to me, and although when I returned to Scotland it was first with Aberdeen, I was very close to re-joining United.

"That was because he'd kept in touch and it made me want to play for him, though on that occasion things just didn't work out."

■ These pictures were taken (left) on Friday, December 3rd, 1971, and (below) on Monday, May 16th, 1983. There are 11 years, five months, and 12 days between the two dates.

It was 4,182 days of innovative thinking, good decisions, but most of all very hard work, that saw the Scottish Premier League Championship trophy come to sit by Jim's desk.

The only thing that didn't change was the Mexico '70 World Cup poster on the wall.

■ Both pics courtesy of Dave Martin, Fotopress.

■ **The immortals. Jim and the 12 Dundee United players who won the 1982-83 Scottish Premier League. (Pic courtesy of Dave Martin, Fotopress.)**

How did Jim spot a good player?

ANALYSIS: STEVE FINAN.

THE ability to identify and recruit youngsters who would mature into being great players is a widely known truth that is always brought up when discussing Jim McLean.

If you look at the 1982-83 championship-winning squad alone, Dave Narey, Paul Sturrock, Davie Dodds, Derek Stark, John Holt, Maurice Malpas, Ralph Milne, John Reilly, Richard Gough and Billy Kirkwood were brought through the United youth academy by Jim McLean.

Hamish McAlpine had been a kid at United too, although before Jim's took the reins as manager.

Paul Hegarty had arrived in 1974, for a fee of £27,500, a 20-year-old striker. It isn't much of a stretch to say he was moulded into the top-class defender he would become by Jim McLean.

Graeme Payne played only eight games of that '82-83 season before going on loan to Morton, but he too was a distinguished graduate of the United academy.

Several of these men went on to play for Scotland. Indeed, in one game, against Israel in 1986, there were five United players on the field in the second half. And Scotland won, 1-0.

Bear in mind, the likes of Andy Gray and Ray Stewart (who would accumulate 30 Scotland caps between them) had come and gone by the time of the championship season, both becoming stars of the top league in England.

The talent-spotting record is truly remarkable.

A lot of these boys were from the Dundee and surrounding area. It was a rich seam of talent that had never been seen before, and certainly hasn't been seen again. And they all came to United. There were very few "prospects" from the local area that joined up at Dens Park in this era. Boys' club managers knew it, school teachers knew it and parents knew it: if you wanted to

■ Right: March 1989. Emerging stars Alec Cleland, John O'Neil, Ray McKinon and Paddy Connolly sign long-term contracts at Tannadice.

■ There are a lot of old United line-ups photos in this chapter. There is a reason for that. Have a look along the rows of faces and pick out the players you know. The ones who went on to "make it". Then take a minute to Google "photos of Scotland schoolboys team". You will find plenty to choose from. Click on any of them from any year. Read the left-to-right captions and see how many names you recognise as having made it to the top of the game. Compare numbers. I think you know what you'll find.

25
40
adidas
36
adidas
36

give your laddie the best chance of a career in football, then plead with Mr McLean to get him signed up at Tannadice.

How did Jim spot all these players?

He had help, of course. Jim is on record fulsomely praising people like Maurice Friel, Denis Gillespie, Walter Smith, Gordon Wallace, Graham Liveston, and Doug Cowie, and many others, for their help in scouting players.

But Jim himself was often seen around the likes of Lochee Park, Drumgeith and Claypotts on a Sunday morning. The more Jim did it (the photo on the right is from his very early days in 1972) the better he got at it.

And when the kids did make it to a United training session, Jim was there to assess them. Jim had the final say, Jim identified the flaws they'd have to overcome to make it as a player, then judge whether the flaws were so severe that they couldn't be ironed out.

How did Jim know these players would become stars?

That's the tough question. There isn't a single answer because it would have been different with every player. Billy Kirkwood had a superb (and often under-rated) ability to mark a man or break up play. Ralph Milne's

■ March 1972. United youngsters. Back, from left: D. Fraser, A. Stewart, F. Esposito, P. Laing, D. Narey, J. Coats, P. Tovey, P. Boyle. Front: C. Scott, G. Payne, J. Murray, J. Spink.

D U F C

natural pace might have been easy to spot, but then fast isn't always good. The ability to head the ball so well might have been instantly apparent in Andy Gray and Duncan Ferguson, but, as with speed, it takes more than one isolated skill to make a player.

Each had talents, but not the same talents. Each had problems to work on.

It comes down to an almost unmeasurable ability to look at a player and decide whether he has "got it".

You can prove a lot of things with statistics these days, and other sports are much easier to measure by stats. But football isn't just about numbers. A team made up of the best, the strongest, the fastest athletes in the world would probably make a decent American Football team with a little bit of coaching, even if they'd never played the game before. The same bunch would be a terrible association football team, though. It would take a decade to make them even half-decent.

Football teams need skill.

And skill needs years of practice with a ball, starting from almost as soon as the child can walk and carried on, every day, every chance that comes up, with a

July 9th, 1973. United kids, back, from left: Andy Gray, Dave Narey, Graeme Payne, Goodall, Murray. Front: Mellon, John Holt, Derek Addison, Gunn.

D U F C
G.P.
B.E
D U F C
D U F C
D U F C
D U F C

■ **August 8th, 1974. United's first team and reserve team pool.**

Back, from left: Pat Gardner, Brian Rankin, Jacky Copland, Hamish McAlpine, Walter Smith, David Narey, Archie Knox, Doug Houston.

Middle: Jim McLean (manager), David Dodds, Brown, Paul Sturrock, Iain McDonald, Goodall, Allan Forsyth, Mooney, White, John Holt, Andy Dickson (physio).

Front: Graeme Payne, Andy Rolland, Duncan MacLeod, Doug Smith, Andy Gray, Frank Kopel, George Fleming, Tommy Traynor.

tennis ball, a beach ball, a supermarket plastic ball, or a Size-5 Mitre Mouldmaster.

Identifying that there is enough skill in a player takes a lifetime of experience in the game.

You have to watch how a player controls a ball, how he makes time for himself. How he moves, how he perceives what is around him. You can scrutinise a player's stats, and he'll look good on paper if he makes 98 out of 100 side-foot passes when he has time to lift his head and play the ball.

It is much more difficult to measure the other two passes out of the 100, when the player is off balance, under pressure, moving at top speed, and the ball is on his "wrong" foot . . . but somehow he still manages to curl a through-ball that is a millimetre out of reach of a defender, but right in the stride of the striker.

Seeing a player do that sort of thing is a good

Right: July 28th, 1987. Dundee United Under-14s cup-winning team.

Back, from left: Graeme Liveston (coach), Gary Bollan, Peter Goldie, Scott Lindsay, Edward Conville, Tommy McMillan, Tommy Rennie,

Front: Colin McKee, Campbell Clark, Simon Stevenson, Christian Dailly, John Lindsay.

July 27th, 1979.

Back, from left: Gerry Leslie, David Dodds, Iain Phillip, Graham, David Narey, Walter Smith, Ray Stewart.

Middle: Jim McLean (manager), Andy Dickson (physio), John Reilly, Craig, Ray Lorimer, Paul Hegarty, Neilson, Frank Kopel, Derek Addison, Ralph Milne, George Fleming, G. Low (coach), Ian Campbell (coach).

Front: Ian Stewart, Paul Cavanagh, O'Brien, Alex Taylor, Derek Murray, Derek Frye, John Holt, Paul Sturrock, Graeme Payne, Ian Ballantyne, Billy Kirkwood.

indication of a good player. But such a situation might only arise once a game, or once every three games.

How do you know if a 12-year-old laddie will be able to do that in a Hampden Cup Final? Well, of course, you don't. And you won't find a formula or a stat that shows you how to do it, either.

But gather the likes of Jock Stein, Bill Shankly, Alex Ferguson and Jim McLean on a side-line and if there is a genuine prospect playing on the pitch then all four of them will have identified which kid it is after three minutes of the game. Indeed, there are tales of scouts saying they took notice of a player just by looking at the way he runs.

It comes down to a gut feeling. Spotting skilful players is a talent, just like being a skilful player is a talent. The ability to point out which kid out of 100 on a crowded, noisy training field is a skill that has to be won through lengthy experience, a detailed knowledge of the game, and that indefinable gut instinct.

The truly remarkable thing about this ability to identify which wee laddie could one day be a Scotland star is that Jim did it for two decades.

Time and time again.

They called it "the Tannadice conveyor belt of talent".

Other managers build one team, or bring through a crop of youngsters all at the same time. Jim found

Jim with Jock Stein. Spotting talent is a talent itself. All the great managers had it.

players year after year, from Andy Gray to Duncan Ferguson, from Graeme Payne to Billy McKinlay.

He also paid transfer fees for genuine quality. Eamonn Bannon, Willie Pettigrew, Dave Bowman, Jim McInally, Ian Redford, Iain Ferguson, there are a lot of names on that list. Indeed, if you look at the Dundee United Hall of Fame (blessed be their names) you'll find that more than 30 of them were players during the McLean era. That isn't a coincidence. It isn't luck either.

Jim could pick a player.

And that Scottish understatement says a great deal for him. But, allied to that, Jim coached all of his players (see page 166) to become better. Much better. And he had an understanding of football tactics that was miles ahead of his time, and has been consistently praised (see any one of the tributes in this book from his players).

One talent, for player-spotting, is a blessing. Two, when you add the coaching ability, is pushing it. Three, if you throw in his tactical genius, is unprecedented.

Jim McLean is the greatest all-round football managing talent that ever trod the streets of Dundee. That's why we call him The Legend.

■ Nowadays they call it "good recruitment". All managers have to make good signings, with clear ideas on how they will fit into and improve the team. Jim signed Jim McInally and Dave Bowman in 1986. (Pic courtesy of Dave Martin, Fotopress.)

adidas
VG

■ Dundee United FC full squad, August 1986.

Back, from left: Brian Welsh, Dave Narey, Richard Gough, Scott Thomson, Billy Thomson, Michael McAdams, Dave Beaumont, John Clark, Bruce Deas.

Second row: Gregor Mitchell, Martin Feenie, Billy McKinlay, Kenneth McDonald, Scott Kopel, Jim McInally, John Bishop.

Third Row: Joe McLeod, Allan Preston, Paul Kinnaird, Kevin Gallacher, Gordon McLeod, Ian Redford, Tommy Coyne, Dave Bowman, Jimmy Page, Gary McGinnis, Paddy Connolly, Ray McKinnon.

Front: Jim McLean (manager), Bill Ramsay (physio), Maurice Malpas, Ralph Milne, Paul Hegarty, Paul Sturrock, John Holt, Eamonn Bannon, Chris Sulley, Gordon Wallace (coach), Ian Campbell (trainer).

VG

■ Dundee United FC full squad, 1988.

Back, from left: Jim McInally, Ian McPhee, Gary McGinnis, Billy Thomson, Scott Thomson, John Clark, Ian Redford, Raphael Meade, Alec Cleland, John O'Neil.

Second row: Gary Mearns, Joe McLeod, Billy McKinlay, Eddy Meenie, David Bowman, Kevin Gallacher, Alan Main, Alan Irvine, Hamish French, Stephen McInulty, John Bishop.

Third row: Gordon McLeod, Harry Curran, Raymond McKinnon, Vince Arkins, Paul McLaren, Brian Welsh, David Beaumont, Paddy Connolly, Mark Perry, Duncan Ferguson, Allan Preston, Scott Kopel, Charlie McKenzie.

Front: Raymond Miquel (shirt sponsors Belhaven) Ian Campbell (coach), Graham Liveston (scout), Paul Sturrock, Maurice Malpas, Paul Hegarty, David Narey, Jimmy Bone (coach), Gordon Wallace (coach), Jim McLean (manager).

BELHAVEN

■ May 1988. The United team that won the Premier League Reserve Cup. Back, from left: Dave Beaumont, Scott Kopel, Scott Thomson, John Clark, Brian Welsh, Harry Curran, Ian McPhee. Front: Gordon McLeod, Alan Irvine, Gary McGinnis, Hamish French, Joe McLeod, Alec Cleland. (Pic courtesy of Dave Martin, Fotopress.)

■ **March 1989. The team for a BP Youth Cup tie versus Hamilton at Tannadice. Back, from left. Duncan Ferguson, Eddie Conville, Stuart Garden, Vince Arkins, John O'Neil, Ray McKinnon. Front: Tommy McMillan, Alec Cleland, S. McNulty, John Lindsay, Gary Bollan. (Pic courtesy of Dave Martin, Fotopress.)**

Momentous news

HOW JIM'S MOVE WAS REPORTED IN 1971:

IT is almost cruel to look back with the full benefit of knowing the consequences of these momentous events at both ends of Tannadice Street in December 1971.

No one then knew how it would all work out. Dundee fans must have been pleased to get the highly experienced former Rangers boss Davie White. The United supporters might not have known too much about their new manager, although reports on what a good coaching job he was doing under John Prentice were fairly common knowledge.

The Sunday Post cutting is perhaps the most telling. It quotes Jim directly and even as early as his second day in the job, you can detect his management style.

Perhaps it was, even then, obvious which club would be the more successful over the next 50 years.

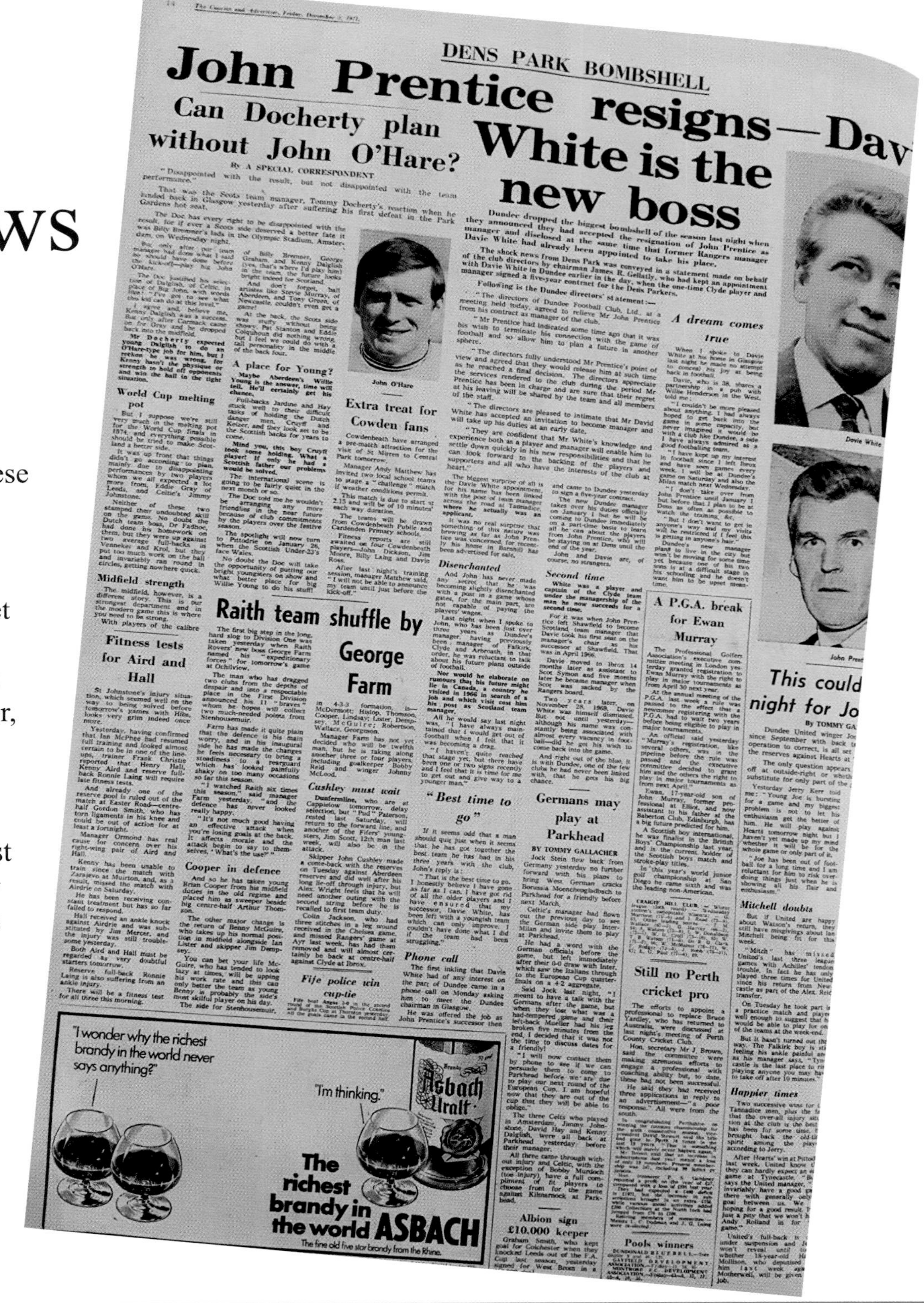

DENS PARK BOMBSHELL

John Prentice resigns—Dav

White is the new boss

Dundee dropped the biggest bombshell of the season last night when they announced they had accepted the resignation of John Prentice as manager and disclosed at the same time that former Rangers manager Davie White had already been appointed to take his place.

Can Docherty plan without John O'Hare?

By A SPECIAL CORRESPONDENT

"Disappointed with the result, but not disappointed with the team performance."

John O'Hare

A place for Young?

World Cup melting pot

Midfield strength

Fitness tests for Aird and Hall

Extra treat for Cowden fans

Raith team shuffle by George Farm

Cooper in defence

Cushley must wait

Fife police win cup-tie

A dream comes true

Disenchanted

Second time

"Best time to go"

Phone call

Davie White

A P.G.A. break for Ewan Murray

Germans may play at Parkhead

BY TOMMY GALLACHER

Still no Perth cricket pro

Albion sign £10,000 keeper

Pools winners

John Prentice

This could be night for Jo

By TOMMY GA

Mitchell doubts

Happier times

■ The Dundee Courier of Friday, December 3rd, 1971.

■ Left, the next day's Courier, Saturday, December 4th. And, below, Jim's thoughts and plans on the job he faced, reported in that weekend's Sunday Post.

The Courier and Advertiser, Saturday, December 4, 1971. 7

Jim McLean leaves Dens for Tannadice

Chairman Johnston Grant and Jerry Kerr welcome Jim McLean to Tannadice.

In full charge of team and tactics

By DON JOHN

On Thursday Dundee lost their manager, John Prentice, and promptly announced the appointment of Davie White.

Yesterday, in a remarkable climax to the Tannadice Street drama, Dundee also lost their coach, Jim McLean, who is moving down the road to become team manager and coach of Dundee United.

The announcement was made at Tannadice Park last night by United chairman, Mr Johnston Grant. The directors were happy, he said, to confirm Jim McLean's appointment. Jim would be in full charge of training, tactics and team selection and is under contract to the club.

Jim will not take over officially until Monday, but he will be with the Dundee United party at Tynecastle today. As I understand he was under contract at Dens, Dundee must have agreed to the move.

In a talk with Jim last night he told me he was delighted with the post, though sorry to leave the players at Dens Park.

"I want to make it absolutely clear," he said, "that I'll be solely responsible for choosing the team, and their tactics on the field.

"I will take full responsibility for United's performance from now on.

"Naturally, I hope the club will go on to achieve success. I'll do my very best, though it could take time to get to know the players' full capabilities, and for my ideas to work out."

Jim has seen United only once this season—and that was when Dundee beat them early on.

Jerry's job

While Johnston Grant and Jim McLean did the talking last night, Jerry Kerr remained quietly in the background.

That's how Jerry wants it in future, although, as general manager he still has an important job to do for the club.

Jim McLean wants no part of the administrative side. He will be able to concentrate on players and play. All the other work of the club will still be Jerry Kerr's department.

It's an arrangement that suits both men and should work out well for Dundee United.

Jerry Kerr, I know, is very pleased with Jim McLean's appointment and he has no intention of interfering in any way. In fact, I would guess, that Mr Kerr is the man behind Jim's appointment.

Shrewd move

It all seems to add up to a shrewd business move by Dundee United. Jim McLean has been a tremendous success as Dundee's coach.

He has ideas and can put them over. He is a strict disciplinarian, a hard man at training, and respected for it by the players.

It's a good move for United—but a hard blow to Dundee.

The appointment of a coach to succeed Jim McLean at Dens would seem to concern new boss Davie White, rather than the outgoing John Prentice.

In fact, last night's move may influence Mr White to take over earlier than originally planned on January 1.

Experienced

Jim McLean, who is 33, gave up a playing career with Kilmarnock to return to Dundee as coach in July last year.

The Dens Parkers had a hard job persuading Killie to release him. Finally they gave full-back Davie Swan in exchange.

Jim's senior playing career started with Hamilton Accies, and from there he went on to Clyde, Dundee, Killie, then back to Dens, as coach.

Brother Tommy plays for Rangers and another brother, Willie, is Dunfermline's coach.

Now, at Tannadice, Jim McLean will do the same job as at Dens, with this vital difference—**he picks the team, and so carries the responsibility.**

But that's the way Jim wants it. It could mean the start of a new era for the Tannadice club—with Jerry Kerr's vast experience still there to add background support to the new team-manager coach.

It will all seem very strange at Dens today

By DON JOHN

What a remarkable afternoon it will be for Dundee players.

As they go into action against Airdrie at Dens Park they will be watched (and still controlled) by John Prentice, who has resigned.

In the stand will be the new boss Davie White—not taking over yet but, of course, intensely interested in the play and players.

Missing from the dug-out will be the man who has worked with the Dens men so closely and successfully—Jim McLean. Jim will be at Tynecastle in his new role of manager-coach of Dundee United.

Maybe it's upsetting for the men on the field, who must feel somewhat shattered by the suddenness of events.

But, as John Prentice said yesterday, "these things are happening all the time in football and are part and parcel of the game."

So I don't think Dundee will get any sympathy if they fail to collect the two points they should win from Airdrie.

As professionals they must have the hard approach. Nothing that has happened off the field must be allowed to interfere with their play on it.

They want a good result today, not only to maintain their promising league position, but to set themselves up for that second leg U.E.F.A. tie against A. C. Milan at Dens on Wednesday.

And, just as important, to encourage the fans to come back on Wednesday.

Frustrating

The Dens Parkers need all the support they can get, not only vocally, but financially. One of the reasons behind John Prentice's decision to give up his football was the never-ending struggle.

"After nearly 30 years in the game professionally," he told me yesterday, "you get tired, and ask—what's the use? What is to be the future for the game in Scotland?

"We now have a promising team at Dens Park, but no matter what they achieve it will not boost the club's income to any great extent. I would say that the recent run of success has only succeeded in halting the decline in Dens attendances, not increased them."

Had enough

Little money to buy, the necessity to sell. This situation applies to so many Scottish clubs at present and the sheer frustration of it is part of the John Prentice resignation.

He still isn't revealing any plans for the future, but it will be **outside** football. He's had enough!

Will he perhaps change his mind after a couple of years away from it all? "Definitely not," said John.

How does his family feel? "They are all pleased," said John, "except my youngest son. He was determined to become a Dens ball boy and now, I'm afraid, that ambition won't be realised."

Steele O K

The Dens pool for today consists of last week's winning team at Dunfermline, plus Robert Robinson, Ally Donaldson and Alec Kinninmonth.

Jim Steele was at the ground yesterday and looks like being available after a touch of flu. Mike Hewitt's knock appears to have cleared up, too.

Team from, Hewitt, Donaldson, R. Wilson, Johnston, Steele, Phillip, Houston, Duncan, Ford, Wallace, J. Scott, J. Wilson, Robinson, Kinninmonth.

Decision on Hall today

Conscious of the five goals lost at Broomfield last week, St Johnstone manager Willie Ormond's main concern will be to evolve a tighter defensive system for the home match against Hibs today.

He could not ask much more from his forwards, who scored four against Airdrie. However, he could hope that they cash in on any early advantage. It was failure to do this which swung the game Airdrie's way and disclosed weaknesses in the Perth defence.

Included in a pool of 13 from which Mr Ormond will make a final choice are Henry Hall and Kenny Aird.

Hall, who has an ankle injury, will be given a try-out this morning. "If he fails this test he will not be included in the Sarajevo party," said Mr Ormond.

Kenny Aird, who has been nursing a thigh strain at the back of the leg, successfully came through a full work-out yesterday. He will be fit for the trip to Yugoslavia and the return U.E.F.A. Cup tie, but may not be risked today.

Meantime, the team will be from—Donaldson, Lambie, Coburn, Rennie, Gordon, Whitelaw, Mercer, Rooney, Pearson, Connolly, Aitken, Aird, Hall.

Ian McPhee, who has been sidelined since the end of October with a knee complaint, makes his come-back with the reserves at Easter Road.

The game will also mark the come-back of forward John Leslie, who has been bothered for some time with leg trouble.

Absent from Saints' second string will be Gordon Smith (knee ligament trouble) and Ronnie Laing (thigh muscle injury).

McPhee is included in the Sarajevo pool and, so, too, is 18-year-old mid-line player Jim Mercer, who has come right into the first team reckoning in recent weeks. He is a product of Grangemouth Y.M.C.A.

16 travellers

The 16 listed for Sarajevo—subject to a clean bill of health after today's games—are: Donaldson, Lambie, Coburn, Rennie, Gordon, Whitelaw, Aird, Rooney, Pearson, Connolly, Hall, Aitken, Mercer, McPhee, Argue, Robertson.

The Perth party will include chairman A. M. Lamond, vice-chairman Bob Sawers, director W. M. Dewar, secretary George Bell and local businessman Eddie Conner, who accompanied Saints to Hamburg and Budapest.

Staying overnight at the Glasgow Airport hotel, the party fly out at eight o'clock on Monday morning with flight changes at London and Zagreb. They arrive at Sarajevo at 4.40 p.m.

On the homeward journey, they leave Sarajevo at 7.20 a.m. on Thursday and are due back in Glasgow at 2.25 p.m.

"I am told the pitch is ice-bound at the moment and am afraid conditions will not be good," said Manager Ormond.

Ally Littlejohn out through injury

Ally Littlejohn, still receiving treatment for a torn hamstring muscle, will miss Brechin City's home game with Stranraer today.

Manager Bob Methven hopes this will be the only one of his players to be ruled out, as he is still waiting to see when Philip Prain (flu), Andy Dow (leg injury) and Brian Reid (injured during training) will be available.

There is to be a private trial at Glebe Park tomorrow.

A £400 cheque is to be presented by Brechin City Supporters' Club at today's game.

Mr David Will, the City chairman, said yesterday that the donation was very welcome and would help to cheer them up during the club's present bad patch.

The money represents a considerable increase in previous donations.

United colts go down fighting

DUNDEE UNITED A 3, HEARTS A 3.

Frances Colliery Golf Club prize-winners—Front (from left)—James Philp (match-play champion), James Wallace (club champion), Andrew Baxter (stroke-play champion), David Philp (runner-up high handicap), Tom Anderson (runner-up match-play), John Dryburgh (runner-up stroke-play), and David Somerville (high handicap cup). Back—William Barclay (club president),

All set for a teaser at Tynecastle

BY DON JOHN

Dundee United go to Tynecastle seeking their third league win in a row.

Victories against East Fife and Motherwell sent the Tannadice team shooting up the table—two more points this afternoon and all earlier disappointments will be forgotten.

Of course the task against Hearts is difficult. Bobby Seith seems to have got rid of the Tynecastle team's "inconsistent" tag. **They've only lost a couple of league matches all season, and now stand third in the table.**

Their most impressive performance was last week at Pittodrie, where they beat Dons in the closing minutes, and with 10 men too! That should ensure a bumper Tynecastle crowd today—all expecting United to be beaten comfortably.

Well matched

The snag is—the Tangerines don't go under easily against Hearts, if past records are judged. It's usually the odd goal that counts and United, with a lot more confidence than a few weeks ago, will make it hard for their opponents.

Jerry Kerr's pool consists of last week's eleven, plus Davie Wilson.

I expect no change in the side, unless Jackie Copland fails to get over an upset that made him feel queezy yesterday.

Ian Reid, in last week's pool, couldn't be considered because of an ankle knock, and Ian Mitchell is still out of action.

Evergreen Davie

If Davie Wilson is called on, it will be the veteran's first appearance since September 25—though Davie has been playing enthusiastically, and well, for the reserves.

Young Harry Mollison looks like getting another outing at right-back, deputising for the suspended Andy Rolland.

United pool—McAlpine; Mollison, J. Cameron, W. Smith, D. Smith, Henry, Traynor, Copland, K. Cameron, Gordon, Stevenson, Wilson.

Hearts will be unchanged. Only doubt was right-back Ian Sneddon, with an ankle injury, but he passed a fitness test yesterday.

Team: Cruickshank; Sneddon, Kay; Brown, Anderson, Thomson; Townsend, Renton, Ford, Winchester, T. Murray.

Farm rings the Raith changes

George Farm, the man who possesses an uncanny knack for transforming Second Division sides into respected top leaguers, begins his bid for the hat-trick at Stenhousemuir this afternoon.

He has transformed Queen of the South and Raith in recent years and Raith fans expect the same result again from him.

He has a no-nonsense approach and is prepared to come down on players who do not give enough.

On the half-dozen occasions Mr Farm has watched Raith this term one thing has stuck out—slack defensive covering.

"This has been prominent almost every time," said the new Raith Rovers boss.

"As a result I have made it my first priority and made changes accordingly."

Cooper switch

The major switch has been the swopping of Brian Cooper from midfield to sweeper operating alongside big centre-half Arthur Thomson.

Thomson, a little slow at times, needs a hard worker beside him to be at his best—Cooper might be the right man, if manager Farm keeps him on his toes.

The other alteration is the reinstatement of Benny McGuire to midfield.

Benny, who has earned the attention of scouts from several top clubs, was out of favour recently with Bill Baxter after one or two off-form performances but the new boss believes his class will prevail and under his direction make him more profitable a player.

The side for Ochilview is: McDermott; Hislop, Thomson; Cooper, Lindsay, Lister; Dempsey, McGuire, Robertson, Wallace, Georgeson.

A substitute will be chosen before the match.

The British Boxing Board of Control have announced that the European Boxing Union have put the proposed European feather-weight championship fight between the champion, Jose Legra (Spain), and Evan Armstrong (Ayr), the British champion, open to purse offers. These should reach the B.B.B.C. by December 16.

Pars look to young Jim

By Don John.

Dunfermline badly need a marksman, and young Jim Scott scored a couple for the reserves against Aberdeen on Tuesday.

Little wonder that Scott is a definite starter at Greenock today. He's tireless, he isn't afraid to have a go, and the Fifers hope that he'll find the right touch again today.

Scott was a substitute in the side last week, when the Pars were under despite a lot of pressure against Dundee.

As confirmation that there isn't a great deal of change he CAN make Alex Wright names a familiar pool of players. Jim Paterson is the only addition.

Paid off

It seems probable that the Dunfermline boss will concentrate on the successful tactics employed at Muirton a fortnight ago. The Pars played it tight—not backs to the wall, but giving nothing away—and earned a good point.

Another away point this afternoon would be very welcome.

Dunfermline team from: Arrol; Callaghan, Mercer, Fraser, McNicoll, O'Neil, Millar, Thomson, Gardner, Scott, Mitchell, Paterson, Gillespie.

Morton list the eleven who won 2-1 at Shawfield last week, plus Don Gillies and Chris Shevlane. Team: Sorensen; Hayes, Laughton, Shevlane, Lumsden, Anderson, Clark, Booth, Mason, Osborne, Gillies, Murphy, Chalmers.

Bannerman's 69 in Florida

Terry Dill, a 32-year-old Texan, who has never won a tournament on the U.S. golf circuit, birdied five of the last eight holes for a seven-under-par 65 at Orlando, Florida, yesterday to take the first-round lead in the £62,500 Disney World open tournament.

One behind him came Dave Eichelberger, Jack Nicklaus, Bob Goalby and two others tied on 67.

The 6924-yard course played easily and 70 players in a field of 144 beat par.

Among those under par on 69 were two members of the British Ryder Cup team, Harry Bannerman and Peter Butler. They are one ahead of Lee Trevino, the year's leading money winner, and two in front of Arnold Palmer and Bruce Devlin.

David Webster hits form in Lagos

Tommy Horton had a seven-under-par second round of 64 in the £10,000 Nigerian Open Championship at Lagos yesterday, to share the halfway lead with Bernard Hunt, who had a 66.

Horton's 64 was matched by American Lee Elder who was in third place on 135.

David Webster, Lundin Links, followed his first round 71 with a fine 65.

Earn Valley Darts League

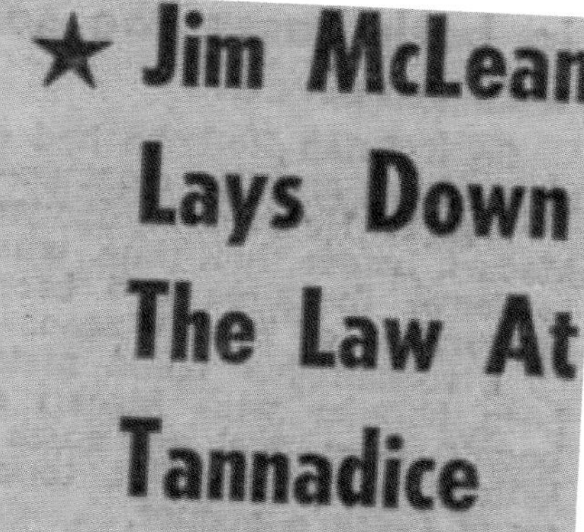

★ Jim McLean Lays Down The Law At Tannadice

DUNDEE UNITED manager **JIM McLEAN** saw his side in action for the first time since they played Dundee in early September. And immediately after the game at Tynecastle he had a long talk with the players, outlining his immediate plans.

DAVIE WILSON and **BILLY GRAY**, who have trained with Partick Thistle at Firhill, and **ALAN GORDON**, who occasionally trains in Edinburgh, will from tomorrow report to Tannadice every day.

"I've also told the players they'll be having extra sessions every Monday and Tuesday afternoons for the next three weeks at least," Jim told me last night. "There's a lot of hard work to be done. I'm going to do my share, so the rest is up to the players.

"I was impressed with what I saw in flashes against Hearts. In fact, I learned more than I imagined I would. The side looks very good going forward, but I'm concerned about the way we lost goals."

Preserving memories of Jim McLean

FAN TRIBUTE: GRAEME WEBSTER, ON BEHALF OF THE ARAB ARCHIVE www.arabarchive.co.uk

THE evening had been charged with emotion. It was eerily silent as the Arab Archive team sidled out of the theatre. The faces of the audience illustrated the journey our former manager had taken us on, all those years before.

The play, *Smile* (see page 240) had rekindled some incredible memories. For 60 glorious minutes, we were thrown back to what now feels like, an inconceivable era. It was a time when Jim was at the helm of our football club. It was a time that each of us, more so than ever, was proud to be an Arab.

As a youngster in the 1980s, my vantage point in Tannadice was the old family enclosure.

It's now converted and renamed the Jim McLean stand. This was a fitting tribute to Jim, particularly as it was a UEFA Fair Play award that funded the previous incarnation. Jim had steered his team to the UEFA Cup final in 1987, against all the odds and as I was lucky enough to be there that day, it now forms an abiding memory of his time.

In the early '80s, on the site of the Jim McLean stand, was a small two-tiered terrace. It was from here I got my first glimpse of the boss.

On match days in the family enclosure we would head down to the trackside wall. With the front of the terrace dipping down below the level of the pitch, our worm's eye view enabled us to get close to our heroes.

We'd be within arm's reach of the likes of Paul Sturrock, one of Jim McLean's most loyal disciples. With tangerine socks rolled down to his ankles and legs shining with newly-applied liniment, we would watch him effortlessly skip down the touchline right in front of us.

ARAB ARCHIVE UNITED IN HISTORY

A glance to the right would reveal the dugout area. I would watch in awe as Jim McLean prowled, barking his orders. He looked a diminutive figure, cut against the vast expanse of terracing behind. I remember thinking that for a relatively small man, he couldn't half shout.

He was our leader and at that time I couldn't imagine anyone else in charge.

As the years progressed, he spent more time out of the dugout than in it. Often in the box behind the technical area communicating by phone. But there was no better sight than the side door bursting open and Jim running down the stairs to scream instructions from the touchline. His appearance would always bring a cheer from the crowd.

Jim was renowned for his tactical genius.

JIM McLEAN

On penning this column for the last time as manager, there is plenty I'd like to say and probably should say, but everyone will have their own thoughts, opinions and judgements of the past 21 years and I have mine, but I don't intend to dwell on them. I'll leave it up to you all to put your own interpretation on my managerial career.

What I will say is how much I appreciate the directors, of whom too many are sadly no longer with us, for taking a real chance in appointing me manager in the first place. As chairman of the club I now appreciate how difficult a time it is and taking someone from Dens only added extra pressure on the board when filling the vacancy. I'd also like to pay tribute to the present directors, particularly Mr George Fox who has had to put up with me the whole time.

For the final match of my 21 years, Aberdeen couldn't have been more appropriate opponents. Encounters with them have produced many outstanding memories. Our first league cup triumph sticks out. Fortunate to get a replay at Hampden, we went out at Dens and thoroughly deserved our 3-0 victory thanks to two goals by Willie Pettigrew and one from Paul Sturrock.

Conversely, we have been on the receiving end too. Their 4-0 semi-final victory at Tynecastle in 1990 being one of the most painful. Frankly, we got a doing that afternoon.

The Dons were also very much involved in the championship race ten years ago. In my opinion three magnificent teams were involved in the three-cornered race for the title, thus making it a very difficult year to win it.

Celtic, whom we narrowly pipped, and ourselves scored a then record breaking 90 goals. It was certainly a season of quality.

Of course it was Aberdeen's recent win at Tynecastle that took all the pressure off us in our last two games as we tried to qualify for Europe. I'd like to thank Mixu Paatelainen for scoring the winner. All the time he was here, he was an absolute pleasure to work with (as I am sure I was to him!)

Accordingly, I wish Aberdeen all the best in the final against Rangers. I sincerely hope that Aberdeen win the Scottish Cup, but **only** because it isn't good for the Scottish game that one club lifts all three trophies.

When you examine the fortunes of clubs of similar resources to ourselves over the past 15 years, we have almost always finished top of that group.

In Europe, however, our record stands comparison with the likes of Rangers, Celtic and Aberdeen not only in number of entries, but also in terms of performance.

Reaching the final of the U.E.F.A. Cup was a magnificent achievement and, in fact, over the past ten years, we have experienced virtually every possible success, bar the acquisition of the trophy which would have been the icing on the cake.

Some of these things (and I hope I am wrong) may never be experienced again.

Looking to the future I wish the club every success in the continued re-development of Tannadice and further improvement on the field of play where the current young crop of players are capable of bringing us more success.

Finally, I'd like to thank the 6,000 or so hard-core of our support who have backed us so loyally through the good and bad times of the past 21 years.

It is how they think of my managerial reign which matters greatly to me, and it has been a privilege to be associated with them.

■ May 15th, 1993. Jim's last ever programme notes as manager. (Courtesy of the Arab Archive.)

I remember, on countless occasions, United coming back from a couple of goals down at half time.

Just 10 minutes with the manager was enough to transform United. He could overhaul hefty deficits with a tweak to formation or a timely substitute. Coming back from 2-0 down to win 3-2 at Ibrox in 1986 springs to mind.

I also loved his mad moments.

Chasing Willie Miller down the tunnel at half-time in a cup-tie at Dens, sticking his best players on the transfer list just to give them a fright, having a dig in the programme at the lack of fans attending games, making the first team play a friendly at Forfar the day after winning the league, and of course, fining players for not being entertaining enough.

I will always be grateful for the memories that he bequeathed us.

He built a team capable of beating the very best in Europe. He demanded perfection from his players and it's only now, upon reflection, you realise he pretty much achieved it.

I hope I'm wrong, but his achievements as manager will never be matched.

The Arab Archive team often reflects upon how lucky we were to witness Jim's teams. We are fortunate to have all these wonderful memories. Not everyone does.

That's one of the big motivations for the work we do on the Arab Archive, we are dedicated to preserving the history of Dundee United Football Club, of which Jim McLean is such an important part.

Jim read games from the first kick

PLAYER TRIBUTE: MAURICE MALPAS.

TANGERINES legend Maurice Malpas rates Jim McLean as the most astute tactician he played for in his long career.

Coming from a man who as well as making an incredible 830 appearances for Dundee United, won a club record 55 Scotland caps, that is high praise.

What makes Maurice's assessment even more special is the fact those games in the dark blue of his country included spells working under two other Scottish managerial greats in the shape of the late Jock Stein and Sir Alex Ferguson.

As big an admirer as he is of those legends, Maurice doesn't hesitate in labelling Jim extra special when it came to masterminding a game plan.

"Jock and Fergie's achievements show they were two men who knew their stuff, but when it came to tactics Jim was definitely the best," he says.

"In setting up a team for a game, and knowing how a game would go, he was out there on his own."

In saying that, the man who won a league championship and Scottish Cup during his time at Tannadice, does not pretend his former gaffer always got things right, but believes that this showed another of his great strengths.

"If a team we came up against did something unexpected, or he felt he'd got his tactics wrong, he never worried about changing things. He would read games from the first kick, so even inside 20 minutes he could move us around.

"There were times, too, when he would alter things just to upset the opposition, doing things they didn't expect. If an opposition player was having a good game, he would put one of us on him and say "take him out of the game for the next half hour".

"There were games where I found myself up the park doing a marking job on someone he'd spotted was causing us problems. Even when everything was going to plan, he'd change things around, just to keep teams guessing.

"For us it was a regular thing to start in one formation, change after 20 minutes, and then change again another couple of times during the game.

"It was something we got used to, and I think it is why, as good as the players we had were, the sum of the parts at United was always greater than the individual talent."

Maurice believes that the tactical flexibility Jim wanted is why he insisted that, with the exception of

■ January 30th, 1999. Jim makes a presentation to Maurice and his family to mark Super-Mo's 800th appearance for Dundee United.

OS
BEST
NEWS &

the goalie, his players were able to perform in more than just one role.

Maurice himself joined the Dundee United youth ranks as a midfielder, before being switched to become a full-back very early on. "In my case I had a nightmare of a game in the reserves against Falkirk and afterward Jim decided to put me to right-back.

"I was part-time at that stage, so Walter Smith and Gordon Wallace used to take me in the evenings and put me through a lot of hard work – I suspect partly because they were none too happy about having to come back in after spending all day training with the full-time boys.

"I played full-back in a youth game and within three or four weeks I was in the first team as a right-back."

Maurice is, of course, best remembered as a stylish left-back, something that was down to Jim McLean's long held belief that his players were footballers first.

"I am naturally right-footed, but Jim never saw that as a reason to keep any player on one side of the park. In the early days, when Richard Gough was the other full-back, I would be handed the job of marking the opposition winger and if he switched sides, then so would I.

"For marking jobs he'd move me into the middle and for him it was a case of if you could only play one position you were no good to him.

"Of the team I broke into in the eighties, everyone could play in different positions and in my time the only positions I didn't play were striker and goalie.

"It was the same for the rest of the team.

"Luggy (Paul Sturrock) was great through the middle up front, but he would also move out wide, and then Doddsy (Davie Dodds) would be centre-forward one

Left: Maurice in February 1978, aged 15, and a pupil at Queen Anne High School, Dunfermline. He had just been selected for Scotland Schoolboys, and was a United S-signing.

week, inside-left the next and usually wide-left away in Europe with Luggy up through the middle."

Never forgotten by Jim McLean were teams and players that certain members of his squad had done well against.

In Maurice's case that saw a history of epic battles to keep wing wizards Davie Cooper of Rangers, and Celtic's Davie Provan quiet.

"Early on I did well against both of them and Jim would give me the job of marking them.

"When I was still part-time he'd even come to me and tell me I was being left out the game before we played Rangers or Celtic to make sure I would be fresh for those games.

"That's the way he was. Every time Jim Bett was playing against us, Billy Kirkwood would be in the middle for us and the two of them would have a right battle and both end up getting booked.

"Jim had an unbelievable memory for details like that. We'd be struggling to remember who we'd played last week, but he'd come to you before a game and tell you about something you'd done well against the opposition a year or two before and that's why, this week, he was using you again in that formation or with that specific task."

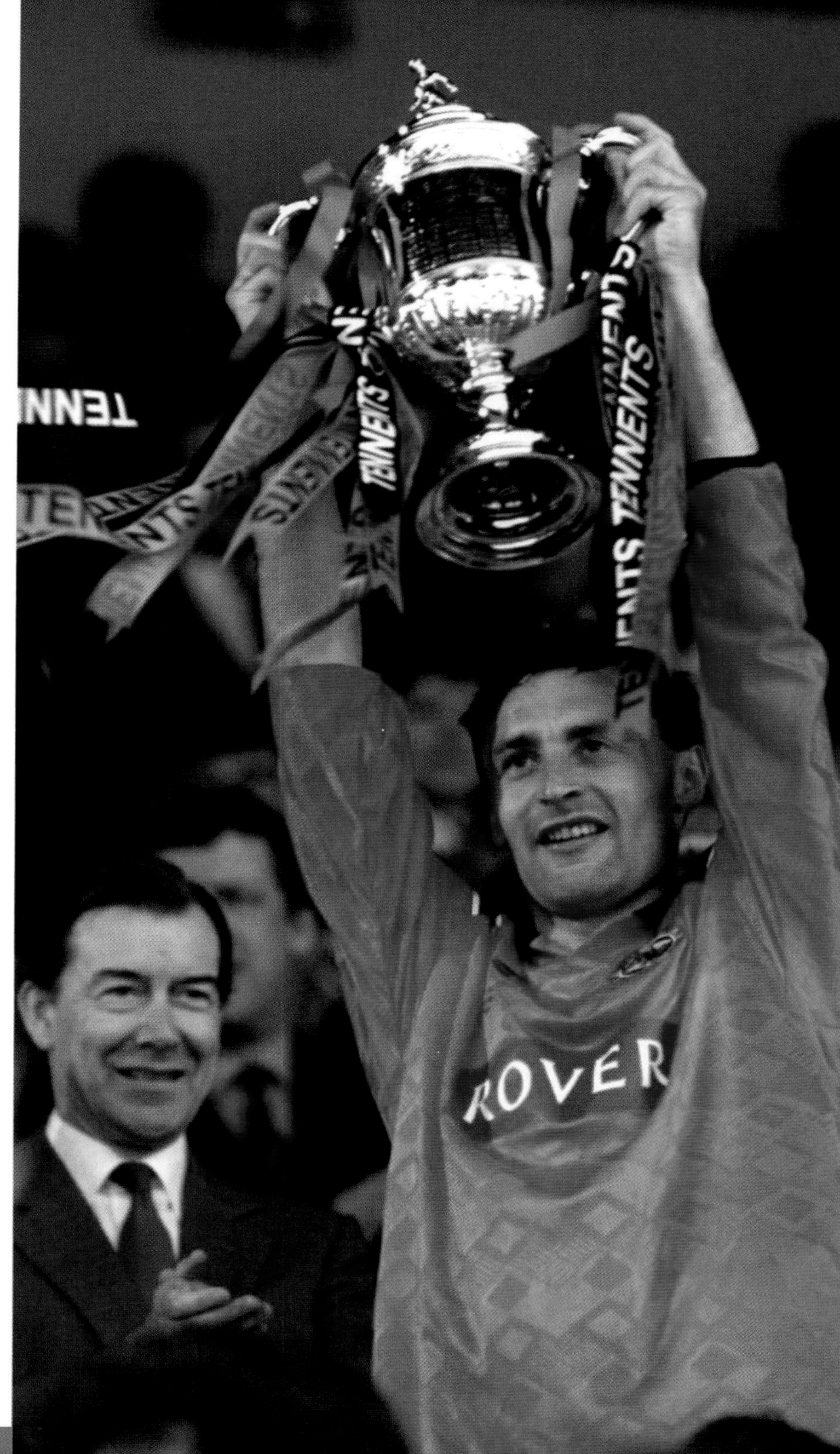

■ As all Dundee United supporters know, Maurice was the first Dundee United captain to lift the Scottish Cup, on May 21st, 1994.

I always have him in my prayers

FAN TRIBUTE: ANONYMOUS.

I DO not wish to leave my name because what I wish to say happened a long time ago and I have forgotten lots of it. But Jim McLean did a lot of work and visited people in hospitals and none of that was in the paper.

He shouted at his players I know that and he got them to play football the very, very best. And he told me about that. And he talked to me a lot and told me lots of things about what he had to do in his work in football. I really enjoyed listening to him and I asked him questions.

I know he is not well now and I am really sorry for that. I wish that he gets better. I always have him in my prayers. I will like the statue and I will go to see it.

FAN TRIBUTE: BRIAN BOARDMAN, ARBROATH.

UNDER Jim's stewardship, Dundee United were transformed into one of the top clubs in Scottish football. Furthermore, their name became synonymous with some of the most feared sides in European competitions. Thanks for the memories, Jim.

The statue is a fitting tribute to a giant of a manager.

FAN TRIBUTE: BARRY FORBES, MONIFIETH.

MY story tells of myself as a 12-year-old boy decked out in the United tracksuit of the time, waiting to be picked up for football training.

I'm sitting on the wall at the garage at the Scott Fyffe circle, waving cheerio to my mum who is heading back to the house.

A gentleman approaches me. He says, "Hello son. Here's something for you." He then passes me a postcard with a photograph of the Dundee United first team, on the back of which contained the signatures of all the players and coaches.

I managed to mumble a few words: "Thank you Mr McLean". As a mark of respect, I would never have called him Jim.

This happened in 1992 and I vividly remember it, each time with a warm smile.

Jim McLean was more than just the greatest manager at my club. He was an inspiration and a hero to the people and had a warm connection with the supporters.

I am eternally grateful for my personal encounter, it illustrates the warm, amiable side of Mr McLean, not often discussed, but always felt by fellow Arabs.

I still have the postcard.

FAN TRIBUTE: BOB HYSLOP.

ONE day my wife and I were leaving Tannadice after a match, having been guests in the boardroom. Jim was leaving at the same time.

The rain was torrential and our car was some distance away. Jim was parked opposite Tannadice.

We had coats but no umbrella. Jim had no coat, but did have an umbrella.

He immediately insisted we take his umbrella, with instructions just to hand it in to Tannadice when convenient.

On several other occasions, Jim, Graham Sinclair (a surveyor) and myself were looking into the possibility of creating indoor football pitches at Gussie Park.

The meetings were always at Tannadice. Without fail, instead of ordering staff to do it, Jim would fetch cups, a pot of tea, and biscuits himself and would proceed to serve us.

I was always struck by his politeness and gentlemanly demeanour.

Jim at a 1987 United training session, having got his brolly back.

Jim McLean is a one-off work of art

TRIBUTE: JIM SPENCE.

ON Sundays in my early twenties, a crowd of us including then United star Graeme Payne, would play a bounce game on the playing fields at Kirkton High. Every now and then Graeme would panic as he thought he saw Jim McLean's car coming into view, and would disappear into the middle of the pitch, and as far out of sight as his magnificent ginger thatch would allow.

It was in its way a testimony to Jim's legendary 24-hours-a-day commitment to the game of football. If he wasn't checking what his stars were up to, he was scouring the pitches around Dundee for up-and-coming talent.

He lived and breathed the game, as an artist might live and breathe painting, or sculpture.

He was a complex character and as a journalist wariness was a handy trait to exhibit in his presence. Yet I never had a serious fall out with him, and he almost knocked me off my chair one night at a boxing dinner, when he turned to me and said simply, "I've always respected you as a journalist". I waited for the punchline, but it never arrived. I can only presume he meant it.

From Jim, not given to dishing out compliments like confetti, it was a rare accolade indeed.

He could surprise you when you least expected it with moments like that. On one occasion I broke a story on live radio about potential investment in United from two Irishmen. The presenter, Richard Gordon, asked me "What's the chairman saying about that then, Jim?"

I didn't have long to wait until I found out. Jim came thundering towards me on the radio gantry to have a not-so-quiet word. The story was in fact true, and in fairness to him, although he'd not wanted it made public, he was perfectly fine with me afterwards.

His depth of knowledge of the game and his rigorous approach to it, took the club to heights undreamed of, and which will never be repeated. His oft-used analogy, of United being the corner shop against the supermarkets, was very apt.

It is, on reflection, absolutely astonishing that he built teams which managed to compete against the best that European football could offer, for so many years. That could never be explained by providence alone: it was down to a wide range of terrific coaching techniques and tactical nous, allied to the ability to spot players' hidden talents and to coax the very best out of them.

When I took part in the recent BBC Alba documentary on United's run to the UEFA Cup final, and the eventual defeat to Gothenburg, Gordon Wallace said when interviewed that Jim had been way ahead of his time, even when a coach at Dens Park.

Whether it was his use of tactical variations which were unusual and innovative, or his embrace of specialist sprint coaches like Stuart Hogg, and seeking advice from Liz McColgan's athletics coach Harry Bennett, Jim was at the forefront of a modernist approach to the game.

His forensic analysis of the opposition was mathematically precise, and he could adapt his team selection and set-up to suit whatever circumstances were thrown at him.

If he had a fault I suspect that deep down it was a lack of confidence in some of his own abilities and decision making; which perhaps sometimes was reflected in United losing matches in which they were better than the opposition.

If that was the case, then he had no need to feel that way. His record stands as testimony to his achievements, in taking a small Scottish football club, consistently, to heights which should have been impossible for them to scale.

He scouted, developed, and produced, over many years, players of top calibre who went on to have a pedigree and career in football on both sides of the Border, which without his superb coaching and tactical ability, they may never have enjoyed.

His was never a nine-to-five world. The game consumed him and enveloped him.

His time as United manager revealed a man with the unique skills to engineer the development of a club, which at one time wasn't even the biggest in its own city, into one which garnered a reputation which has stood the test of time throughout the football world.

When will we see his like again? Never is my guess. Like the Mona Lisa, Jim is a one-off work of art.

126
AWAY

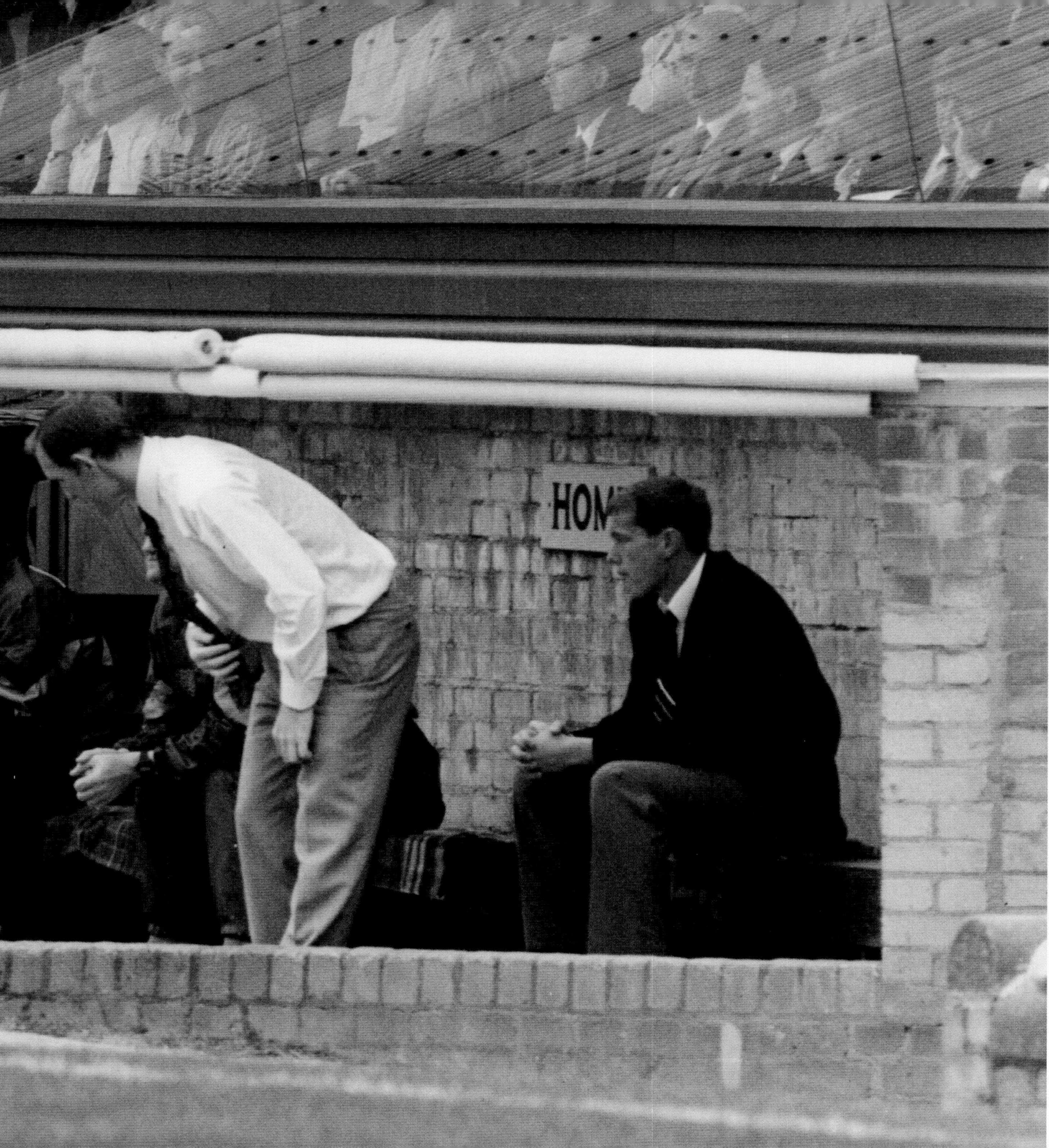

■ This is how all United supporters remember Jim McLean.

He talent-spotted fantastic players, trained them to be even better players, sent them out to play with innovative tactics, and prepared for every game in minute detail.

But the bit that the fans saw at matches was that he drove his teams on by his sheer strength of will and force of personality.

There will never be another Jim McLean.

You're wanting money AGAIN?

FAN TRIBUTE: VIKKI OGILVIE.

I WAS part of the Wee Jim's Tangerine Army supporters club and Doris and Jim would always come to our end-of-season Player Of The Year dance.

Because I was one of the youngest, I'd get the job of selling the raffle tickets.

Every time we got to Jim he would always say, "I can't believe you're wanting money AGAIN from me this year."

But he would still buy five strips of tickets every time, and if he ever won he'd always tell us to re-draw the prize.

Then another time, me and a friend were going to watch a pre-season game against Forfar and waiting at the bus stop at the bottom of the Forfar Road.

I saw Jim's purple car go past and I was raging he didn't stop for us.

Next minute, my pal said: "Is that not that purple car coming back down the other side of the dual carriageway?"

Right enough, here was Jim and Doris in the car picking us up.

But Jim always said that it was Doris that made him do it!

FAN TRIBUTE: COLIN WESTWOOD.

THE most memorable thing about Jim McLean, for me personally, is what Jim said to my dad.

If you watch the video clips from Dens '83, at the full-time whistle a fan runs on to the pitch . . . and is swiftly removed by two policemen.

Jim has a word with him as he is marched back into the enclosure.

That pitch invader was my dad!

As the police marched him back across the track Jim went to him and said: "Don't f****** spoil it!"

My dad was the first man Jim spoke to after we won the league at Dens!

Right: Dens Park 1983: Colin Westwood's dad is helped back into the crowd, after securing his unique place in Dundee United history!

CONSTITUTION ST
PETROL

A safe and positive place for families

TRIBUTE: SUZANNE BOSLEM, OF THE TELE'S SUE SAYS COLUMN.

IN the 1990s, I had a weekly column in the Dundee Evening Telegraph called Sue Says. I wrote about my life and views and being an avid Arab and Tannadice season ticket holder.

I regularly wrote about United, but from the point of view of a fan, not a sports journalist. I never critiqued the game or players. Instead I wrote about things that affected me: everything from the state of women's toilets at Scottish football grounds (minging, although Tannadice was an exception) to tripping over my handbag at a match, to being excited ahead of big games. Things people could relate to, even if they didn't agree with the column's unashamedly tangerine hue.

I wrote this stuff, never thinking I'd have to answer for any of it. One day, the Tele's sports editor Ed Gorrie shouted across the office that Jim McLean was on the phone. I laughed and told him to stop mucking about. But he insisted.

Right enough, it was the legend himself. I'd supported United since I was a kid, all through Jim's glory years. This was a big deal for me.

He told me he liked my column and invited me to Tannadice to meet him and a few of the players.

On the day, I was excited, but a bit scared – he had a reputation and a few of my colleagues had been on the wrong end of a rant.

Sure enough, he showed me a drawer of every press cutting he deemed offensive. It was a big drawer. "But you're never in there," he said. Phew! There was no hairdryer – he was kind, interested in my work and generous with his time.

He invited me to join a committee he'd set up looking at how to get more women and families to come to football. We looked at how to present the club as part of the community and a safe and positive place for women and families. It was still unusual for women to be in the stands and he knew I was taking the club out of the sports pages to a wider audience. I was good PR before anyone really knew what PR was! Jim was greatly ahead of his time with this.

I wouldn't say I got to know him well, but I enjoyed my time on the committee. He and Doris gave me a lift home a few times. A particular highlight was a trip to Ibrox where he gave us a behind-the-scenes tour. My auntie still talks of the time I saw him at Celtic Park and he shouted: "All right Sue?" and gave me a wave across the car park like I was an old friend.

I found him to be an old-school gentleman with a great sense of humour and remember him fondly. I'm grateful I got to spend some time with my hero.

Jim never lost sight of who was important, who the hard work was for. Dundee United fans. (Pic courtesy of Dave Martin, Fotopress.)

THE CITY OF DUNDEE
The Lord Provost and Councillors of the District of the City of Dundee
JAMES YOUNG McLEAN
Chairman and Managing Director of
Dundee United Football Company Ltd.
AS AN HONORARY BURGESS OF THE CITY
Chairman and Managing Director of Dundee United Football Company Ltd
the Councillors and Citizens
Lord Provost
Chief Executive

Jim McLean — Dundonian

HE was born in Larkhall, a Lanarkshire boy, and raised in Ashgill. But Jim McLean is the most famous Dundonian in living memory. No one else has done so much to spread the name of the city across Britain and the Continent.

Dundee City Council recognised this in 1993, by making him an Honorary Burgess, more recognisably referred to as "given the freedom of the city".

The "coonsul", as we call them in the toon, don't do this often. The Queen Mother, and The Black Watch, were honoured in 1954, but in the past 50 years it has been given only eight times. Usually it is awarded to a political figure from outwith the city, such as past Labour Party leader Ramsay MacDonald or (controversially) Aung San Suu Kyi of Myanmar. Locals so honoured include former lord provost Maurice McManus and Dundee Parish Church minister William Macmillan.

No one connected with football had ever been made an honorary burgess before.

Jim was proud of this. The oval-framed award hangs in the hallway of his home in Broughty Ferry to this day.

The council like their football teams to do well, of course. Success generates spending and elevates the standing of the city. But they don't hand out "freedom" for just one trophy or a few good performances over a couple of seasons. It goes beyond that.

This is an award that is above football. This was given because Jim McLean added a value and a cross-borders currency to the word "Dundee" that it would not, could not have gained had it not been for him.

It is a thing that everyone in Dundee should be thankful for, no matter which team they follow, because it benefitted all Dundonians.

The wording on the document reads: ***The Lord Provost and Councillors of the District of the City of Dundee met and convened as Council and having the Lockit Book of Burgesses opened before them DID and HEREBY DO, in pursuance of a Resolution so made, admit and receive JAMES YUILLE MCLEAN, chairman and managing director of Dundee United Football Company Ltd., as Honorary Burgess of the city with all the rights, privileges and immunities belonging to a Burgess of the District of the City of Dundee, and with the full powers to exercise the same in recognition of his long, distinguished and valuable service as Manager and subsequently as Chairman and Managing Director of Dundee United Football Company Ltd., and his great interest in the development of Premier and European Grade Football in the City and in testimony of the esteem in which he is held by the Councillors and Citizens.***

■ 1993. Tom Mitchell, Lord Provost of Dundee at the time, presents the honour to Jim.

Continent-wide respect

TRIBUTE: STEPHEN GETHINS, INTERNATIONAL LAW SPECIALIST AND FORMER MP.

I HAVE been a Dundee United supporter as long as I can remember. My cousin was five years older and his tangerine propaganda was firmly embedded from a young age. It meant that, throughout my childhood, Jim McLean on the touchline was as much a fixture of my life as anything else. The passion and the expectation that the team would give its all regardless of the opponents.

That helped when I got to school. We were football daft, a game was played before the school day started, during morning playtime, as soon as a quickly scoffed piece was finished at lunchtime and in the afternoon break. Every moment that could be spared we kicked a ball about.

It also meant that there was a focus on how everyone's team was doing. At school in Perth in those days everyone seemed to be a Celtic supporter. The school's priest even said a prayer for our opponents before one of the, what seemed like, many cup finals we lost to them in the 1980s. After the May Cup final weekend I always seemed to be the one in charge of holding the door open for everyone as my triumphant Celtic-minded schoolmates trooped through the doors.

There were up-sides. Our team's success was unique. The European runs that we could talk about excitedly, giving me unprecedented street credibility as United beat team after team from across the rest of the continent.

Stephen has lived and worked all over Europe, specialising in arms control and democratisation in former Soviet bloc nations.

Sitting with my wee brother watching the game on a black and white that had an aerial, Mum was watching something else in the living room. Hajduk Split, Lens, Barcelona – all places I would later work in but would always be special to me.

Jim McLean taught us that we could stand proud in Europe and that legacy lives on.

When I worked in the European Union, football was, for many, the common language. Everyone knew about Dundee United and they knew the name of Jim McLean. His achievements put us on the map.

He gave us that pride that we can achieve anything, be up there with the best. It doesn't matter who everyone else supported, Jim McLean gave the team and the rest of us the self-confidence to stand out.

November 26th, 1986. Jim McInally scores the first during United's 2-0 win over Hajduk Split, his first goal for the club.

Compete with confidence in Europe

TRIBUTE: ELLIS WATSON, CHAIR, TAY CITIES ENTERPRISE FORUM

THE very idea of the Tay Cities Deal is built on a sense of place. A recognition of what the Tay Cities area is, what is has been and what it can be, is fundamental to what we are doing. We want success for our area. We want to be winners. We want a future in which we fully realise the potential of the Tay Cities area and the people and businesses in it.

It's obviously a very different playing field, but we recognise the parallels between what it takes to create a winning football team and what it takes to create a winning team of innovators, creators, and businesspeople. Teamwork, helping each other, scoring victories, and collectively being the best we can possibly be. We need every member of the team to perform well.

Jim McLean is an excellent example of a man who had a plan for the way he wanted his organisation to function, put a structure in place to allow success to happen, and motivated his team to reach their full potential.

The people of the Angus, Dundee and Perth areas identify strongly with football, whichever team they follow. A winning football team stirs a civic pride that elevates the way people regard themselves and how they feel about the place they come from.

If we can do as well on a national and European scale as Jim McLean did with his great Dundee United teams of the past then we'll allow ourselves to call it a success.

Because we feel that the Tay Cities area is well equipped to compete with confidence on the European stage, just as Jim McLean's teams competed well, made friends and won admiration across Europe.

The fact that the UEFA Fair Play Award was invented in 1987 to recognise the sporting behaviour of the crowd at Tannadice Park says a lot for our people.

The UEFA executive wanted a way to reward the ovation given to the away team, IFK Gothenburg, who had just beaten United in the 1987 UEFA Cup Final.

That award still exists, and is given to a new recipient every year. It is a European tradition that started here in the Tay Cities area.

Mr McLean's teams brought Europe-wide attention to our area. Football-aware people from the Urals to Iceland know what Jim McLean achieved. That recognition can only help when inward investment is sought.

The whole Tay Cities region can be proud of the achievements of Jim McLean, one of our own.

■ **Jim McLean with the 1987 UEFA Fair Play Award.**

UEFA

A lesson on how to deal with people

FAN TRIBUTE: STUART McMILLAN, EX-MONIFIETH, NOW EDINBURGH,

BACK in the late 80s/early 90s, whilst a hormonal teenager with a Tannadice season ticket, I used to frequently write to Jim (by letter, no emails in those days) to point out where the club was going wrong and give him the benefit of my worldwide scouting experience (gained from my bedroom reading of *World Soccer* magazine!)

On one occasion, Jim's interest was obviously piqued by something I'd said or he was fed up receiving my letters and wanted an end to it! Either way, he invited me in to his office one Saturday before a game.

I got myself a shirt and tie, and tried to look as respectable as possible.

He met me very courteously and said he'd already been to Motherwell and back that morning for a funeral. With that on his plate, and a match to prepare for, he still found time to sit down and talk to a young fan about the future of the club, signings, and financial imperatives.

He spent an hour with me, listened patiently, and asked if I had any ideas for generating more income or increasing crowds. And, if so, to put my thoughts on paper and send them in.

He even took the time to ask about my little sister who, at the time, was in the Young Lions. At the end of our meeting, he took me out to trackside, shook my hand, hailed a steward, and asked him to show me to a good seat in the stand to watch the match.

A couple of years later, after a match at Kilmarnock, the United team bus was leaving Rugby Park and I happened to be walking back down the road. There was Mr McLean in the front seat and, seeing me, recognition crossed his face. He looked straight at me and gave me a wave of acknowledgement.

I'll never forget the graciousness, courtesy and patience shown by the great man in taking the time on a busy day to sit down and speak to a youngster and listen to his views. It is something that taught me a humble lesson about how to deal with people, an experience I was so grateful for and will never forget.

FAN TRIBUTE: PAUL BRUCE.

WHEN I was eight years old I was standing outside Easter road waiting for the players to come out after the game.

Jim came up to me and asked if we would like to go on to the bus and meet the players. He was such a gentleman.

Great memories.

FAN TRIBUTE: RICH WALKDEN, EX-DUNDEE, NOW YORKSHIRE.

JIM McLEAN was my hero growing up and still is today. He made me believe that my team could be the very best and that supporting United was everything.

His passion and drive gave us all something to believe in, a cause to follow. And, very importantly, the lessons about what can be achieved through hard work have stayed with me into my adult life.

I met Jim once, on May 15th, 1983, at Forfar — the day after THE day. I remember it as though it was yesterday. I was seven at the time and hanging about the dug-out at Forfar, with a lot of other kids desperate for autographs. I remember meeting Paul Sturrock, who wasn't playing, and getting his autograph. I spoke to Mr McLean before the game and he shook my hand.

I always wanted to meet him as an adult to say thanks for the memories.

Throughout my career I have continually referenced the values and ethos of Jim McLean when challenging, pushing and developing both students and staff alike. He valued hard work and self-discipline. These attributes are what I look for in others.

As the head teacher of Ecclesfield School, I am in a privileged position to help shape the personal and character development of young people at the most crucial time in their lives.

One of the biggest barriers for students is resilience. Mr McLean had this in abundance and instilled this in his players as they took on the "big boys" across Scotland and Europe. He wasn't prepared to accept excuses and made sure they were prepared for the battles ahead. This is the same as preparing students for the outside world.

People and society have changed, but the core values of success, and achieving it, haven't.

FAN TRIBUTE: STEVE JACK.

UNFORTUNATELY, I have never met Jim (they do say "never meet your heroes") however, I hold him in such regard that perhaps actually meeting him would have been a step too far for me.

But I would like to pay my own tribute.

He was the greatest manager Dundee United have ever had. His record speaks for itself.

But the fact that it was achieved by a "corner shop" club makes it all the more incredible. He put Dundee United, and therefore the city of Dundee itself on the map in European terms, to the point that they are still known everywhere.

His footballing and tactical nous was second to none – and I include Sir Alex Ferguson in that.

I thank Jim every day for the heights he took my club to, and the memories he gave me. I look forward to seeing his statue.

Here's to wee Jim!

Those red cards for Mrs Thatcher

TRIBUTE: LYNNE SHORT, DUNDEE CITY COUNCILLOR.

MY dad took me to Tannadice when I was a toddler. Mum worked shifts so he either took me to the football, or babysat me. The football won, which I am very thankful for.

This was the 1970s and, as a youngster, it was the smells I remember. Pie and Bovril aromas wafting out from the shop – and other smells from the gents at the back of the terracing.

I used to sit, legs dangling, on the wall at the corner, above the TSB Bank advert.

I quickly became hooked, of course. I was a season ticket holder before long. I absolutely loved everything about going to Tannadice.

Into the '80s, my favourite player was Eamonn Bannon. When he ran by on the wing, just a few yards away from me perched on the wall, you could smell the liniment on his legs. It is still a favourite smell for me.

And we lived in Invergowrie, not far from Hamish McAlpine. Sometimes we'd see this local hero in the street.

I grew up and spread my wings, as young folk do. I became a tour guide in Europe.

One of the tours used to be from Switzerland, where I was based for a while, to the principality of Monaco. I was the only guide who could say that I had actually seen the by then tragically dead Princess Grace in the flesh. I'd seen her at Tannadice, of course.

There was always someone who was a football person, and I'd speak to them, no matter where they were from or how halting their English was. They spoke the international language of football and they had always heard of Dundee United. Jim gave us that fame.

And following Jim McLean's United provided one of the sparks that ignited my interest in politics. I was at the Scottish Cup Final of 1988, when Margaret Thatcher attended, and supporters in both ends held up red cards and sang in unison about what, exactly, she could do with her poll tax.

Football is an important part of Dundee, that's one of the reasons I think the statue is such a good idea. It reflects that this is a football town. No matter which team you support, there is always a discussion you can have about the game.

Even today, you can see that it runs right through the city. United are always happy to send players along to talk to teenagers about not being dafties. That sort of thing gets through to them.

I was helping at a dinner for the homeless on Christmas

■ **Jim's Dundee United gave Lynne (right) first-hand experience of Princess Grace (above, with Prince Rainier at Tannadice). Sort of.**

Day and United's managing director Mal Brannigan was there serving up the food, along with his children.

He didn't make a big thing of it, just got on with it. It was a big-hearted thing to do and is another example of the way Dundee United has become woven into the fabric of our town.

But United wouldn't be such a big and famous and good-going concern today if it wasn't for Jim McLean building the foundations of success and creating the modern structure of the club.

A great man. He deserves to be remembered for ever.

Jim's fame spread to North Yorkshire . . . thanks to Panini stickers

TRIBUTE: DANIEL GRAY, AUTHOR, BROADCASTER, SOCIAL HISTORIAN.

I STILL have it today. It is stacked on a bookshelf so that at any moment I might pick it up, open its pages and travel 30 or so years into the past.

Panini's *Football Sticker Album 89* declares the title above a graphic of (to use match report parlance) a despairing goalkeeper.

Pallid sticky tape clasps the spine, just about holding the album together, and thready veins are strafed across the cover.

It is from another time, a bygone age.

Down the left-hand side are paraded the crests of the English and Scottish football leagues, and the PFAs of both nations.

To a young boy living in North Yorkshire, the presence of these Caledonian symbols was beguilingly exotic.

Their inclusion represented the fact that this album had spaces for stickers of Scottish teams; that after the name Wimbledon came a new beginning: Aberdeen.

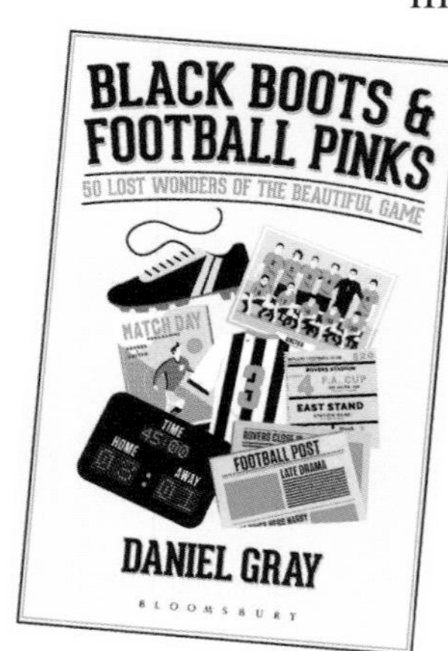

Dan is the author of: *Black Boots & Sporting Pinks: 50 Lost Wonders of the Beautiful Game.*

In 1989 Scotland was merely a concept to me, and Scottish football enticingly "other" and, well, foreign.

It was, then, this very album which lifted me and so many other young English collectors into the world of Dave Smith's clownish head, Malcolm Murray's absurd mullet, and the wonderfully glamorous name Campbell Money.

Moreover, it introduced us to legends of the Scottish game, names we had only heard in passing on *Grandstand* or *Saint and Greavsie.*

Names like Jim McLean.

Of the 12 Dundee United stickers on offer in that 1989 Panini book, I am still missing three of them (Maurice Malpas, Hamish French and Kevin Gallacher, if you have spares). I have the DUFC team photo, and the 'shiny' club badge sticker – always prized – and I have the Jim McLean sticker.

Looking at that photo of him now, I remember looking at him then.

I was struck then, as I am again, by the warm grin of this genial grandad type.

Surely a man with his benevolent smile

and demeanour would be incapable of the serious, grumpy sergeant fibres needed to oversee a successful football team… ?

"One of the longest-serving managers in Britain", reads the profile beneath McLean's sticker, "…assistant manager at Dundee Football Club before taking over at Dundee United in 1971."

Above it, Club Facts announce, in stately print, some of the truths about McLean via the listing of Honours – I was able to decipher that the Premier Division and League Cup (twice) had been won during his reign. This was my kind of mathematics.

Thus was my young vision of Jim McLean formed by a sticky piece of paper.

It took moving to Scotland some 15 years later for me to learn that this man deserved an entire sticker album to himself.

Panini, after all, had said nothing of Roma or Barcelona. No single sticker could convey the fact that mention of this man's name leaves some Dundonians weak at the knees.

It is a name that seems to belong in a thesaurus, rather than a sticker book; a term with hundreds of meanings, all of them joyous to those who wear the tangerine and black.

Jim looks like a "genial grandad", Dan reckons. (Pic courtesy of Dave Martin, Fotopress.)

Jim McLean is not just a hero to Dundee United fans, he is a deity

TRIBUTE: BRIAN TAYLOR, THE BBC'S POLITICAL EDITOR, SCOTLAND.

JIM McLEAN, eh? Memories, memories, magnificent, gargantuan, exuberant memories. Of triumph and trophies. Of glory. And, if you will permit, a little personal reminiscence too.

I started supporting United out of sheer badness. My family – a substantial posse of uncles and cousins – all followed another team who played, I believe, in dark blue.

In a spirit of youthful rebellion and enabled, indeed encouraged, by my tolerant father, I opted for the Terrors. My United allegiance developed around 1962 or '63. Followers of that other team will recognise the significance of the dates.

At this time, I was an eager young pupil at Blackness Primary in Dundee. For the avoidance of doubt, that is the real Blackie. Not the present Blackie – which is the Hackie, in disguise. Look, get a Dundonian of a certain vintage to explain.

From the Blackie, I went to the High School.

Same problem there. Surrounded by adherents of the Dark Blues.

It took a certain chutzpah to back United then.

But, even in those early years, things were looking up. Firstly under Jerry Kerr, with his pipe and car coat, himself a fine manager.

He brought us victories – including, gloriously, the Dens Park Massacre of '65 – when United won five-nil (and the team in dark blue fielded a certain J. McLean.)

On that day, Finn Dossing scored a hat-trick for the Terrors. Years later, I inducted him into the United Hall of Fame.

The Mighty Finn told the rapturous audience: "I have played for several teams in my career. But there has only ever been one club for me – and that is Dundee United." There wasn't a dry eye in the house.

Under Jerry Kerr, a first foothold in Europe. Barcelona, Juventus.

And then, finally, to Jim McLean. Quite simply, one of the finest managers in Scottish club history, up there with the likes of Jock Stein and Alex Ferguson.

I revere Stein, Ferguson and others. Their achievements are huge. But perhaps Jim McLean merits particular praise in that he built a winning side at a club that had so little in the way of triumphant history as a bedrock.

His achievements were gigantic, overwhelming. He was a brilliant football tactician. Determined, diligent and dedicated. Utterly, obsessively committed to success.

That level of compulsion generated some criticism. But the fans simply loved him for it. I had the pleasure of interviewing Philip Differ, who wrote the play *Smile* about Jim for the Rep. Did he realise, I asked, that Jim McLean was not just a hero to the fans? He was a deity. It was (slightly) tongue in cheek, of course, but, with mock solemnity, Phil readily agreed.

The stories. That Jim told the club, when he arrived, that the only equipment he needed was a stopwatch. Because he planned to make the players run and run and …

But, countering that apparent simplicity, the tales of focused coaching. Individual players saying that the boss drew their attention to small but significant flaws in their approach.

Perhaps with subtlety. More often in rather blunt fashion. Either way, he worked and worked with them until they were better players.

The famous tale of the game against Motherwell. United were 4-1 up at half-time, adding two more in the

Brian, like Jim, has been honoured by The University of Dundee.

second half. The manager was ecstatic, wasn't he? He was jumping for soccer joy, right?

Well, up to a point. He docked part of the players' bonus because he felt they were "insufficiently entertaining" in the second half. One can only imagine what the players thought of this maverick move (actually, no imagination necessary: I've heard some of them on this and other topics related to the boss.)

But, be clear, the fans loved him all the more for this all-consuming dedication to the United cause.

He drew together a quite outstanding team, honing and driving them. His United won the League Cup in 1979. At Dens. Against Aberdeen. A particular delight for me as I was working as a journalist in the Granite City at the time – and thus gained bragging rights.

Then we repeated the feat, thumping our dark blue opponents. At Dens.

Other cup finals. Displaying potency and fight but lacking ultimate success. Still a story of dedication.

And Europe. Not just once or twice but in successive seasons, a prolonged, persistent narrative of endeavour.

The semi-final of the European Cup in 1984, robbed by Roma. The final of the UEFA cup in 1987 when we valiantly and gallantly applauded a lap of honour by our victorious opponents, Gothenburg.

But most Arab minds, I guess, will turn first to the League Championship. Incredibly, brilliantly, luxuriantly, we won the League.

In 1983. At Dens. The day the ball soared over Kelly's head – and it was Happy Birthday Ralph! The day Eamonn knocked the ball home. The day of triumph. And Jim McLean. Smiling, carried shoulder-high by the team.

Supporters of the side in dark blue had a fanzine entitled Eh Mind o' Gillie, reflecting their admiration for Alan Gilzean. They are right to reflect on that great team – and I salute them for it.

But eh mind o' Hamish the Goalie, the great McAlpine. And Derek Stark, and Maurice Malpas, and Richard Gough. The wonderful duo, Paul Hegarty and Davie Narey. Of Bannon, Milne, Billy Kirkwood, Paul "Luggy" Sturrock and Davie Dodds. Of John Holt and John "Boney" Reilly.

I salute them – and all the other heroes who played for United. In the McLean era. And before. And since.

Over the years, I have had the pleasure and privilege to meet Jim McLean on several occasions. I welcomed him on stage at the Caird Hall in 2009, for our Centenary.

Later, in 2015, I inducted him into the United Hall of Fame. I described him then as a "colossus" and a "managerial genius".

My sentiments have not changed with the passage of years.

"Incredibly, brilliantly, luxuriantly, we won the League at Dens!"

CONSTITUTION
HOME

A statue that will stand for all time

THE JIM McLEAN statue will still be standing proud at Tannadice in 200 years' time. This is the start of what will become a piece of Dundee history. Your grandchildren's grandchildren will look at it and wonder "Why is there a statue to this man?"

They might have to look through the history books (or history holograms, or whatever unimagined technology they'll have) to discover more about this bronze figure. They might wonder why United supporters touch Jim's toe for luck (as I'm sure will become a United tradition).

They might wonder, who put that statue there? The Jim McLean Tribute Group, with helpers, put it there.

The erection of statues is a rare thing in Dundee. It might well be argued that we don't celebrate the sons and daughters of the city enough.

Even more remarkable is that the money to erect this statue was raised by public subscription. There were significant donations from companies, and the football club themselves were very generous too. But in the main this was paid for by Dundee United supporters via online donations or other fund-raising initiatives, not least bucket collections at United home games.

And this is where the real power of this lies. The statue is a fans thing. It is they who are marking the fact that Jim McLean dedicated his life to the club. The supporters are the most important people at any club. Without them, there is no club. They got organised to raise money for a statue to the foremost "great" of Dundee United's history.

Crucially, the statue has the blessing of Jim's wife Doris, and his family. Any statue will always create differences of opinion. Some might argue over the pose, the size, the placing, the plinth, the material used. Some might say that Jim should have been portrayed as a younger man, or at the end of his reign as chairman.

Doris was involved at all levels. She agreed to do this because she knew that the first approach about a statue had been made several years ago to Jim himself, who had given an OK. It is that knowledge that prompted her to give the go-ahead to this incarnation of the idea.

Doris likes the statue. And if she likes it, then no one else can say otherwise. She knew him best of all.

To United supporters, past and present, this is a thing to be proud of. This statue represents a great period of our club's history, and depicts a great man. It will speak to future fans. It will tell of the traditions of the club, and the regard the fans will always retain for those who made the club what it is today. No matter the highs and lows that football brings, this statue will represent a man, but also the place Dundee United holds on all those who have tangerine blood in their veins.

Jim McLean was the most tangerine of us all. We are United in our respect for his achievements.

■ Statue Steering Group members Anne Petrie, George Haggarty, Claire Leslie, and Audrey MacGillivray, with the maquette, raising funds at the 2019 DUFC Open Day. Special mention should go to George, who played a difficult and very important role in the process, and who also did an awful lot of work. He skilfully liaised between the club, Jim's family, the Press, the steering group, the sculptor, and all who contributed money or work – keeping everyone in the loop at all times. When approached to chair the group, he would have had no idea of the scale of the task he was being asked to take on, but saw it through with dignity and diplomacy. George deserves recognition and thanks from all United supporters for his part in making the idea of a statue into reality.

Get the best, get the memorials guy

THE STATUE: ALAN HERRIOT.

FOR those of us who know little, or even less, about sculpting, sculptures and sculptors, there is one golden rule that should be followed when selecting an artist you can trust to make the concept of a tribute into reality: go to the guy who is asked to do war memorials.

Because war memorials are always dignified. There is a touch of majesty about them. Few people think "experimental art" when they want to pay their respects to heroes or to an iconic figure.

The Jim McLean Statue Steering Group chose Alan Herriot.

Alan Herriot is one of Britain's finest figurative sculptors (figurative sculptures, I have learned, are those that represent the visible world). He graduated from Dundee's Duncan of Jordanstone College of Art in 1974 and was mentored by Scott Sutherland, who created the world famous Commando Monument at Spean Bridge and the emotive Black Watch Memorial on Dundee's Powrie Brae.

Alan has followed in his footsteps. His works include Wojtek The Soldier Bear, in Princes Street Gardens, Edinburgh; the Royal Army Medical Corps Memorial in the National Memorial Arboretum, Staffordshire; and the WW1 Black Watch Memorial in Ypres, Belgium, among many others. One of his more touching projects was Bamse (Norwegian for teddy bear) the sea dog, mascot of the Free Norwegian Forces in the Second World War. There are identical statues of Bamse, one at Montrose Harbour, one at the quay in the port of Honningsvag in Norway, facing each other across the North Sea.

There could be no one better than Alan to create a memorial to oor Jim.

Alan welcomed me to his studio, not far from Penicuik in the Lothians. He's quite a guy. A polymath who sculpts, paints, writes, plays the piano to concert standard, writes his own musical pieces and designed (and built) his studio and home, which is a like-you-see-on-the-telly sort of place.

He explained the intricacies of getting a bronze of the greatest ever manager in the city of Dundee on to a plinth.

"I worked from a couple of good photos," Alan said, "Though not as many as I would have liked. Despite the two-dimensional photos I had to see Jim in a three-dimensional way, and he had to be portrayed as he was in 1983. That was the brief, because that is when the Championship was won, but it made it just slightly more difficult. Getting his profile was the most crucial bit. I had a few snatches of TV interviews of that era to help, although he turns quite quickly in them.

"Luckily, I could also make use of some of the older or newer footage than the 1983 stuff, as the shapes of foreheads and noses don't change quickly. Hairstyles were different in the 1980s, of course, the fashion then was for longer side-chops.

"I'd also looked to get some movement in the piece, which can be difficult when we are dealing with what was a posed shot for photographers. And it has to have that indefinable quality of "being Jim".

The statue has received the ultimate accolade, the seal of approval from Doris, Jim's wife. She was visibly moved when she first saw it, recognising the pattern of veins on his hand, the wedding ring on his finger. She declared it a fantastic likeness of him.

Alan continued: "The trophy was particularly difficult. These sorts of things are rarely portrayed in sculptures, but it was an integral part of the piece."

The statue is 110% natural size. Alan explained that sculptures are very rarely done at life size. They are put on to plinths, usually at least a couple of meters high, so to maintain proper perspective the subject has to be slightly larger. It's an art thing.

The thing that is striking about Alan is his enthusiasm. He isn't a United supporter, but having played a bit is a football bloke and he has grown to be highly respectful and rather fond of Jim McLean.

He is also proud to finally have an example of his work unveiled in the city where he attended art school and has come to also hold a pride in "getting it right".

He has an artist's perspective on this, which will be different from supporters but which fits well with the ultimate aim. He knows how much this man means to so many people, and he responds to that by taking an immense pride in the work. He was at pains to capture the Jim McLean that we all knew.

Alan Herriot.

And it works. His art does the sculptor credit and its subject credit. This is a statue that all United supporters can properly take pride in.

■ Above: The various stages of statue creation in Alan's studio, from the armature (the framework all sculptures must start with), to fairly late on in the process.

The championship trophy was created separately and added in.

■ Right: The two photos of Jim that Alan used most to work from.

They show him during the correct era, in or around 1983. They are, of course, two-dimensional images and are lit differently, taken from different perspectives and magnifications, which illustrate the size of the task of creating a three-dimensional sculpture from them or from any photo. No measurements could be taken, or walk-around views could be had.

Also inset is the full-sized clay version, before it was taken to the foundry and a cast of it created, which forms the mould for the finished bronze statue.

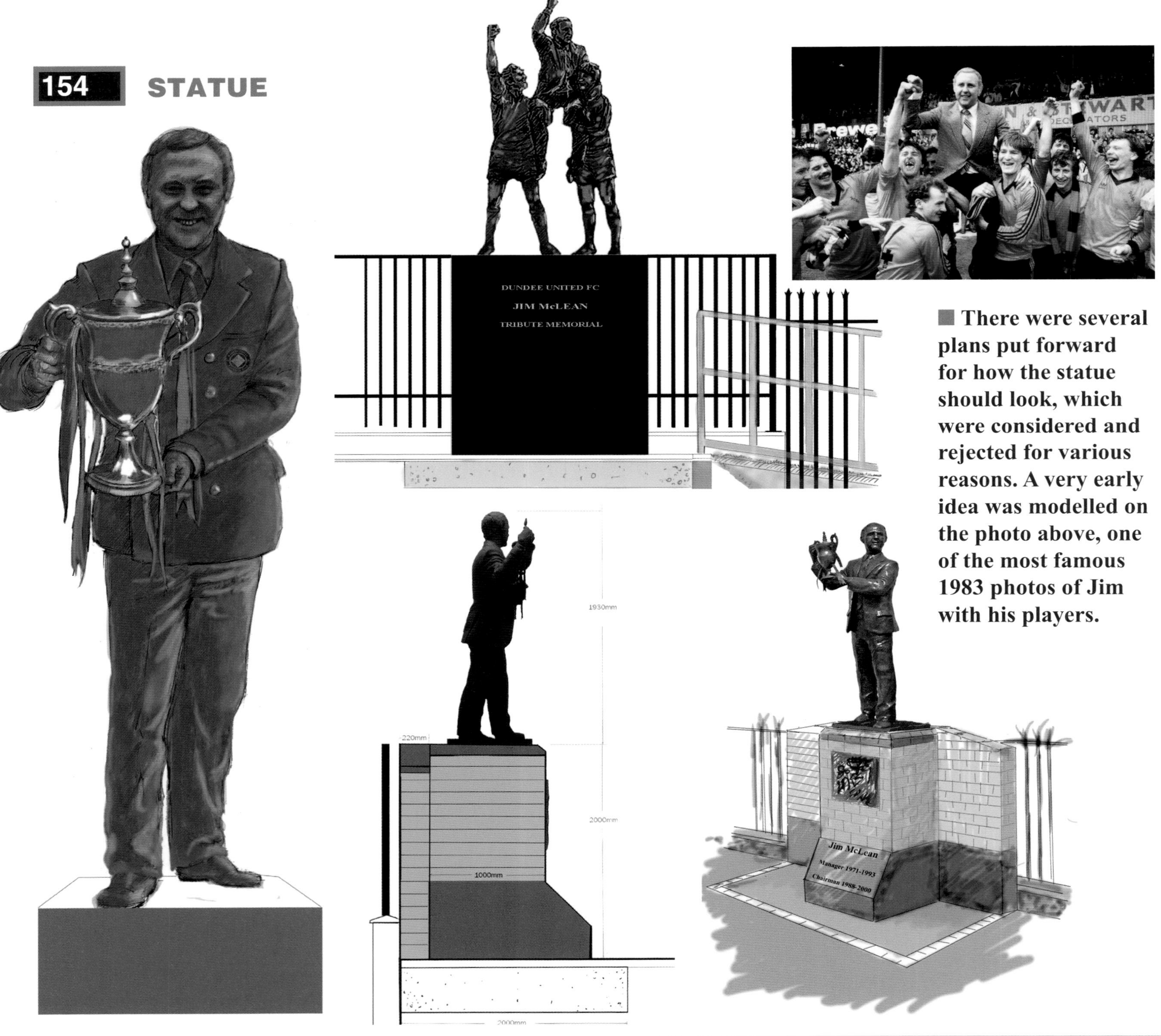

There were several plans put forward for how the statue should look, which were considered and rejected for various reasons. A very early idea was modelled on the photo above, one of the most famous 1983 photos of Jim with his players.

Transportation

NORMAN JAMIESON LTD

THE transportation of the statue was done by Norman Jamieson Ltd, who are shirt sponsors and long-standing supporters of Dundee United.

Lynne and Stuart, who run the company, have been United supporters all their lives, as was their father Norr, who sadly died in 2019. The family are Tangerine through and through, proud owners of the ball with which Nadir Ciftci scored the third goal in United's famous 3-1 win over Rangers at Ibrox in the Scottish Cup semi-final of 2014.

Getting the precious statue cargo from the foundry in Edinburgh and putting it in place on its plinth, was no small, or easy, task. It was a precision job that took time and care, but was gladly donated to the cause.

On behalf of all Dundee United supporters, a big thank you goes to Norman Jamieson Ltd.

Groundwork

CARMICHAEL & BAXTER GROUNDWORKS LTD

THE groundwork and creation of the plinth on which the statue stands was done by Carmichael & Baxter Groundworks Ltd, based in Cupar.

This was the single biggest donation to the statue fund. The original target for the siting of the statue was above £70,000 but Peter Carmichael's generous gesture, undertaking to construct the concrete founds and the preparation work required, reduced that by a five-figure amount.

It's quite a gesture, quite a mark of respect. Peter is an ardent United supporter.

On behalf of all Dundee United supporters, a big thank you goes to Carmichael & Baxter Groundworks Ltd.

■ The Statue Steering Committee were at pains to pay tribute to the generous donations in kind by the firms above. The work undertaken by these companies, which would otherwise have cost a great deal of money, stands as a mark of respect, and a measure of the esteem the owners of these companies had for Jim McLean.

Those who made Jim immortal

I PUT a request to the Statue Steering Group to pay their own tribute to Jim. Some preferred to remain behind the scenes, but I am grateful that several gave me their thoughts.

In the years and decades to come, the statue will stand at Tannadice, and Jim will be remembered. But it is the nature of a shifting world that those who worked so hard to make it happen might be forgotten. But that doesn't lessen the work, or the achievement. The group of people who got together deserve recognition. They have made Jim McLean immortal. They are Dundee United heroes.

STATUE STEERING GROUP TRIBUTE: GEORGE HAGGARTY.

I WAS privileged to chair the hard-working Jim McLean Supporters' Tribute Group. Jim stands alongside the golden generation of Scottish Managers: Jock Stein, Alex Ferguson, Matt Busby, and Bill Shankly. The modern game is still building on the foundations those men laid.

Alan Herriot worked closely with us at every stage of the design and production of the statue and we are grateful for his great enthusiasm and creative skill. Doris McLean has given us tremendous support.

The statue celebrates the historic achievements of Jim McLean and his players, and challenges the club as to what the future holds.

All fans can take great pride in this permanent tribute to Jim McLean.

STATUE STEERING GROUP TRIBUTE: CLAIRE LESLIE.

I'VE been a United supporter since I was four and for many years only ever knew Jim as our manager.

No one since has done what he did, no manager has put out a team that can play like his teams did. I will always be thankful for what he made Dundee United into.

I met him once. I'd seen him a few times in the Ferry, but had never talked to him. He has his "Jim McLean aura". Then one morning I saw him and Doris in Brambles Cafe, having a coffee, and plucked up the courage to go over and simply say: "Thanks for everything you did for Dundee United." He was gracious and polite and a lovely man.

And that's what the statue is for. He devoted so much of his life to Dundee United. He must have spent every hour of his day thinking about United.

A statue is the least we the supporters can do to repay him for all the time United took him away from his family.

I'm proud to have been involved.

STATUE STEERING GROUP TRIBUTE: DAVID DORWARD.

IN European, UK and Scottish footballing terms Jim performed a miracle that will never be seen again.

When he became the manager of Dundee United in 1971 he inherited a club which had never won a national honour, and from the outside was seen very much as a small provincial club.

The club had had only one player, Orjan Persson, capped for their country. Within a few years of Jim's appointment David Narey became the first Scottish Dundee United player to be capped. There is a wonderful photograph with Jim and six of his players all in their Scotland strips.

The team saw a consolidation in the First Division under Jim's leadership and of course in 1979 and 1980 we won our first silverware with the Scottish League Cup.

Even then, the fans could not have dreamed how high their club would reach. Winning the Premier Division in 1983 for the first time was incredible.

Under Jim's management the club's achievements in Europe were simply awesome. If that story had been told in *Roy Of The Rovers* it would have been seen as fanciful. From 1976 United were 14 consecutive seasons in Europe, made it to the European Cup semi-final and UEFA Cup Final. The ties with Manchester United, Barcelona and Borussia Monchengladbach were memorable.

Jim was a manager of his club for 22 years, an incredible achievement, and then of course stayed on as a director and chairman for a further nine years.

He is simply the greatest and most loyal manager a Scottish Football Club has ever had.

The statue is a long overdue recognition of Jim McLean's achievements. The fans raised £62,000 in a relatively short period, and this in itself represents the strength of feeling they have for Jim. The Statue Group have always been sensitive to the wishes of Jim's family.

STATUE STEERING GROUP TRIBUTE: MIKE BARILE.

I'VE been very supportive of this project for many years. It blossomed into a very successful achievement, whereby ordinary fans raised the bulk of the funding.

On a personal note, I love what Jim McLean has done for Dundee United, our city and Scotland. Although demonised by the west coast media, especially for rejecting the top job at Ibrox, he continued to successfully challenge the Old Firm. He took our "local corner shop" and challenged the "top supermarkets" of UK and Europe. However, Tannadice suited him and he suited Tannadice. I doubt if he could have achieved as much elsewhere. The time and place were a perfect match.

His tactical awareness and innovative methods stretched most of his players to breaking point because he always wanted his teams to reach their best and touch perfection. Although he lost far too many cup finals, the journey was unforgettable, full of joyful triumphs.

We are blessed to have had him. He gave supporters so

many fantastic memories and I, like thousands of Arabs, wish to honour and thank him for the glory years.

STATUE STEERING GROUP TRIBUTE: ANN PETRIE.

JIM McLEAN is part of my youth, from my Dad giving me a hoisty-over at the turnstiles, to making Jim cry with laughter when interviewing him for a school project.

This came about when as a school kid in 1982, I'd chosen the topic "violence on football terraces" as my modern studies project and had written a set of questions to all the Premier League clubs. Tannadice phoned one Saturday (after having just been beat one-nil fae Kilmarnock), asking if I'd like to meet and interview Jim. Thrilled and awed at age 14, I trotted along on a Monday lunchtime to quiz him.

My first jokingly-asked question was what went wrong on the Saturday? I was treated to a complete dissection of the game.

I made the point we would've done better if the injured George Fleming had been playing. He snorted an "aye right" response, then we did the rest of the interview. At the end I again asked as to George's readiness for the next game, which got a: "Is he really your favourite player?"

When I said yes he sat back and, honestly, he cried with laughter. When he recovered he asked if I'd like to meet him? "Hell yes!" I replied and we trotted through Tannadice, eventually getting to where the players were having lunch. Jim shouted out for George to come over and then announced, "Well George, I always told you, somewhere out there there'd be someone. And here she is". Then he walked off leaving me, a genuinely star-struck teenager and a somewhat embarrassed, but lovely, George Fleming staring at each other.

Growing up in the eighties in Dundee wasn't always easy and supporting United wasn't always a joy. But Jim gave me, my family and best friends the most amazing memories that are part of who I am.

Jim never got anything like the recognition he deserves. To this day he is someone I think the SFA would rather hadn't been around, unless he'd been part of the Old Firm — in which case he would have already had a statue.

To get the opportunity to be a part of making this a reality is an honour.

I'm proud of the response from United fans. When doing the bucket collections at the Inverness and Dundee games, I loved that a lot of kids handed over their coins especially considering they wouldn't have really known him. Fans sought us out so that they could contribute, it was important to them to know they played a part. We also got donations from Inverness fans, mainly older ones who had fond memories of him.

We often got comments from United supporters such as: "The club should've paid for this". We never agreed with this, (though the club have been very supportive throughout). We wanted this to come from the fans. He belonged to us and this was our opportunity to say thank you, Jim McLean.

Not many kids from Scotland get to talk about gubbing

Barcelona, Borussia etc. Jim, you and your magnificent league-winning, Europe-conquering players have made us known around the world.

This is our way of saying thank you for all the memories, for the world-class players and, of course, thank you for the midfield general and his white boots.

STATUE STEERING GROUP TRIBUTE: DENIS McGURK.

IT was a pleasure to be involved in the fundraising to raise a fitting tribute to Jim McLean. It is just a small token of appreciation for the memories and life experiences enjoyed during the Jim McLean era.

Jim's exploits at home and across Europe were a sporting phenomenon, and not only put Dundee United on the football map, they strengthened Scottish Football's global reputation. He captured the imagination of neutrals and raised the profile of the city, leading to visits by supporters from places across Europe and beyond, allowing them to discover everything Dundee has to offer.

I recall with great pleasure the club's first major trophy, then retaining the League Cup the following season; winning the league at Dens; blowing away the likes of Barcelona and Borussia Monchengladbach to reach the UEFA Cup Final; and coming to within 90 minutes of a European Cup final.

Not forgetting the occasion when five of his players played for Scotland in the same game.

It was clear to me that Jim McLean has every right to join other footballing greats such as Bill Shankly, Jock Stein, Sir Matt Busby, Sir Alex Ferguson and Brian Clough in having a statue raised in recognition of his contribution to football.

The wonder and adventure created by Jim McLean's managerial genius is due full recognition.

STATUE STEERING GROUP TRIBUTE: PETER McBRIDE, TANNADICE DISPLAYS.

IT was a great honour to be part of the Jim McLean Tribute Group from the very outset, when we met to discuss how to proceed in meeting the fans' wish for a statue to be erected at Tannadice.

We interviewed five sculptors and decided on Alan Herriot, who has been an exceptional choice. Now that the statue is in place hopefully all United fans will enjoy visiting the ground and getting selfies with Jim.

As a dedicated fan starting out in the early 1960s I had no reason to believe that we would ever win a cup let alone be Scottish Champions!

When Jim crossed the road to take his first and only managerial role we could not have expected to have won four national trophies before he departed Tannadice.

Jim's legacy is the number of football players he brought through to the first team, with many going on to coach or manage teams when their playing careers ended.

Statue fund online donors

MORE THAN £60,000 WAS RAISED FOR THE STATUE, MUCH OF IT BY DONATIONS MADE BY FANS. TAKE PRIDE. THE DONORS INCLUDED:

4M Accountants
A Doran
A90 Arabs Society
Adam Brown
Adam Lawson
Adam Wilson
Aidan Croll
Alan Costello
Alan McFarlane
Alan Paterson
Alan Robb
Alasdair Duke
Alex Bird
Ali Murray
Alistair Brown
Alistair Penman
Alistair Sinclair
Allan Carver
Allan Lee
Allan O'Rourke
Allan Preston
Allan Webster
Alyth G.C.
Andrew Fleming
Andrew Maclennan
Andrew Scobbie
Andrew Stephen
Andrew Stirling
Andrew Taylor
Andrew Welsh
Andrew Winton
Andrew Zimmermann
Andy Clark
Andy Hannah
Andy Holt
Andy McAdam
Andy McCarle
Angus Housing Association
Anna Hemings
Anne Milne
Anne Petrie
Anthony Notarangelo
ArabTRUST
Archie Logan
Arthur Harris
Arwen Elder
Asda Kirkton
Audrey MacGillivray
Audrey McFadden
Balmore Bar
Barry Ewen
Barry Forbes
Barry Galloway
Ben Laird
Ben Whiting
Billy Ramsay
Bob Robb
Boomerang
Brian Colgan
Brian Edmonds
Brian Hassan
Brian Kearney
Brian MacKay
Brian Ness
Brian Simpson
Brian Stewart
Broxters Boxers
Bruce Henderson
Bryan Orr

Bryan Wylie
Callum Anderson
Calum King
Calum MacBain
Carmichael & Baxter Groundworks
Carnoustie Golf Links
Carol Morrison
Carol Preston
Celtic Football Club
Charles Cranmer
Chris Batten
Chris Chambers
Chris Kinnear
Chris Martin
Chris Matheson-Dear
Chris O'Rourke
Christopher Hepburn
Christopher Taylor
Cinnamon Restaurant
Claire Leslie
Club 83
Colin Clement
Colin Dick
Colin Stewart
Colin White
Colum Deignan
Connor Warden
Craig "Smudge" Smith
Craig Carr
Craig Lindsay
Craig Logan
Craig Simpson
Dads and Lads
Dane Vannet
Dave Holmes
David Abernethy
David Arrenberg
David Browning
David Connor
David Dorward
David Grant
David Haggart
David Hales
David Hamilton
David Hill
David Lonie
David Lowe
David Mitchell
David Rennie
David Syme
Dawn Lambie
DCA
Dean Kettles
Dean Milne
Denis McGurk
Dennis Webster
Derek and Helen Crossan
Derek Duthie
Derek McLaren
Derek Mulholland
Derek Walker
Dominic Stewart
Don Michele Restaurant
Doug Logan
Douglas Jack
Douglas Rew
Douglas Scully
Douglas Sloan
Drumoig Golf Club
Duncan Crighton
Duncan Maynes
Duncan Munro
Dundee United Business Club
Dundee United Football Club
Dundee United Supporters Foundation
E Gurvan
East Angus Arabs
Ed Parkhouse
Elaine Perschke
Elizabeth Agathe
Ellen Searle
Euan Gow
Ewan McFarlane
Ewen Allardyce
Fans United
Federation of Dundee United Supporters Clubs
Fiona Lammond

Forbes of Kingennie Golf Club
Fortes
Frank Fotheringham
Frank's Auto Centre
Fraser Christie
Fraser Jackson
Fraser Low
Fraser MacLeod
Fraser Page
Fraser Sturrock
Frews Bar
G Stark
Gair Souter
Gareth Dickson
Garry Lees
Gary Cassidy
Gary Glancy

Gary Kell
Gary Watson
Gavin Dodds
Gavin McAinsh
Geoff Kennedy
George Anderson
George Haggerty
George Malcolm & Son Ltd
George Mather
George Shannon
George Smith
George's Barber Shop
Gillian Clark
Gordon Barrie
Gordon Grady
Graeme Lawrence
Graeme Macphee
Graeme Petrie
Graeme Wilson
Graham McLelland
Graham Ritchie
Grahame Conning
Grant Montgomery
Grant Stirling
Greg Fairweather
Greg Lawson
Greg Munro
Gregor Kennedy
Gregor Nicolson
Gregor Stephen
Greig Bryson

Grossi Dry Cleaners/Ferry Launderette
Grossi's Dry Cleaners
Grouchos
Hannah Baillie
Harjinder Bhachu
Heather McKenzie
Helen Breen
Helen Docherty
Hollister Ltd
Howdens Kitchens North Muirton
Hugh Rooney
Iain Craig
Iain Dingwall
Iain Ferguson
Iain Meiklejohn
Iain Sharp
Iain Shaw
Iain Stirling
Iain Strachan
Iain Tasker
Iain Thomson
Iain Whyte
Ian Hogg
Ian Hunter
Ian McIntosh
Ian Mckinnon
Ian Mitchell
Ian Ross
Ian Thomson

Indigo Hotel
Isla Cameron
Islay Reid
J Blair
J Linton
Jack Bruce
Jack Inglis
Jack Searle
Jake Clark
James Clarke
James Finnie
James Higgins
James McDonald
James McGeary
Jamie MacDonald
Jamie Macdougall
Jane Brogan
Jenni Amos
Jennifer Amos
Jigsaw Media
Jillian Carroll
Jim Devlin
Jim Freeman
Jim Gardiner
Jim Howie
Jim Reid
Jimmy Fyffe
Jimmy Young
Jo Jack
Joan Sinclair
Joan Sinclair & Glenn Andrews
John Bennett
John Craig
John Hally
John Hamilton
John Hughes
John Lindsay
John MacIntosh
John Maillie
John Miller
John Robertson
John Symon
Jon Knoyle
Karl Russell
Kay Sievewright
Keith Sym
Keith Wilson
Ken & Ryan Smith
Ken Anderson
Ken Boyd
Kenneth Anderson
Kenny Campbell
Kenny May
Kevin Campbell
Kevin Jones
Kevin McCluskey
Kevin Quinn
Knock Castle Hotel and Spa
Kristofer Mellis
Kristopher Auld
Kurt Herx
Kylie Anderson
Laura Conway
Lawrie Low
Leanne Maillie
Lee Harrow
Lee McLean
Lee McLeish
Lee Rankine
Lee Stewart
Leigh Edwards
Leslie Simpson
Lien Wollep
Linda Fletcher
Linda Walker
Lindsay Scott
Lord Provost of Dundee
Lorna Officer
Lorraine Robertson
Louis Kinsella
Louise Adams
Lynn Mitchell
M Gauld
Mackie Motors
Malcolm Macgregor
Mandy Monaghan
Maria Brannan
Marie Kiernan
Mark Baruffati
Mark Cox
Mark Dorward
Mark Dunwoodie
Mark Grace

Mark Jamieson
Mark MacDonald
Mark Ramsay
Mark Riddock
Mark Waterson
Martin Gordon
Martin McKay
Martin Pankhurst
Martyn Smith
Master Steedman
Matt Miller
Matthew Sime
Mechars Mex
MHA Henderson and Loggie
Michael McDonald
Michael Spence
Mick Lees
Mike Barile
Mike Donnelly
Mike Orobczuk
Mike Ramsay
Millars of Broughty Ferry
Molly McGurk
Morag MacLeod
Morgan Steel
Morris Forbes
Mr Walker
Mrs Lynn Coleman
Nathan Graham
Neil Brown
Neil Dyer
Neil Forsyth
Neil Galloway
Neil Gellatly
Neil Hallyburton
Neil Jardine
Neil Lowdon
Neil Lumsden
Neil McCulloch
Neil Robertson
Neil Smyth
Neil Stoneman
Nicholas Hughes
Nick Heaver
Ninja Kiwi
Norrie Bremner
P Sutherland
Pat Nolan
Patricia Smith
Patrick McCarron
Paul Bellamy
Paul Bruce
Paul Enterkin
Paul Gorman
Paul Morris
Paul Naysmith
Paul Rooney
Paul Wynne
Pete Bell
Peter Anderson
Peter Carmichael
Peter McBride
Peter Norris
Peter Thom
Phil Martin
Philip Agathe
Philip Dunlop
Philip Emery
Philip Martin
Philip Scott
R MacFarlane
Ray Martin
Raymond McFarlane in honour of Ron McCutcheon
Richard McBride
Richard Millar
Richard Mills
Richard Sime
Richy Gray
Ricky Ross
Ricky Smith
Risquest Safety Consultants
Ritchie Dorward
Robert Graham
Robert Nicolson
Robert Thomson
Roddy Adam
Roger Wallace
Ron Edgar
Ron Reid
Ronald Fyfe
Ronnie Coull
Ronnie Sievewright

Ronnie Young
Room 39
Ross Archbold
Roy Mason
Ruth McCarron
Ruth Ogilvie
S Thoms
Sara Willison
Scotscraig Golf Course
Scott Cargill
Scott Carnegie
Scott Deuchars
Scott Donnachie
Scott Duncan
Scott Foran
Scott Laing
Scott Walker
Servant Print
Shabir Aslam
Sheena Hird
Shona McKinnon-Whitelaw
Signature Signs
Sir Alex Ferguson
Slaters Menswear
Snug Bar
Stanley Pietrzyk
Stephen Buick
Stephen Dempsey
Stephen Finnon
Stephen Gellatly
Stephen Goold
Stephen Kearnan
Stephen Watt
Steve Arkle
Steve Dempsey
Steve Kell
Steven Balsillie
Steven Boath
Steven Drake
Steven Ford
Steven Leahy
Steven McCarron
Steven McDonald
Steven Mckay
Steven Reid
Steven Sheehan
Steven Watson
Stewart Haddow
Stewart Mason
Stewart Mcculloch
Stuart Balfour
Stuart Campbell
Stuart Fiddes
Stuart Jamieson
Stuart Lenney
Stuart Reid
Stuart Tilston
Susan Batten
Susan Doull
Susan Keilloh
Suzanne Gill
Tayprint
Tele Taxis
Tesco Kingsway
TEW Printers/Terry Walls
The Robertson Clan
Thorntons Estate Agency
Tom Cairns
Tom Gauld
Tony Deans
Valerie McGurk
Vanessa Cobb
W MacFarlane
West End Butchers
William Ritchie
William Smith
Willie Pettigrew
Wilma Boyington
Wilson Family
Yvonne Taylor

Many more fans contributed anonymously and through collections at Tannadice and other fund-raising events.

Warmest thanks to everyone who contributed so generously to this wonderful tribute to Jim McLean.

Jim McLean Supporters' Tribute Group

Doris McLean and family

Jim McLean, football coach

ANALYSIS: STEVE FINAN.

JIM McLEAN was allowed to walk out of Dens Park, where he was forging a reputation as an innovative and up-and-coming coach, with radical ideas on how the game should be played.

Even the most diehard Dee would admit that this was a mistake.

From Jim's own recollection, there were strong rumours that manager John Prentice was going to quit Dens and Jim knew that he didn't get on with the father and son team, the Gellatlys, who ran Dundee FC at the time.

Prentice, had to, as Jim puts it himself, "act as a buffer" between coach and boardroom. The Dens Park manager's post, Jim realised, probably wasn't going to be his.

But Dundee's loss was United's massive gain. The Tangerines got a coach who would go on to prove he could do amazing things

Jim as Dens Park coach. This photo was taken on July 27th, 1970.

Sell to

with a little backing, some time to recruit his preferred type of players, and to create a proper scouting network and youth football structure.

But what makes a good football coach?

As has often been said, Jim McLean liked his teams to keep possession. The idea was to have a solid defensive line – Gough, Hegarty, Narey, Malpas, for instance – who could always be relied upon to use the ball well, and always be sure to be in position.

All attacks were built from that secure foundation, and it must be said that Jim's teams attacked with pace and flair. A forward unit that usually contained Paul Sturrock, Ralph Milne and Eamonn Bannon contained both guile and searing pace.

The midfield had to work hard, very hard. Billy Kirkwood, often overlooked when fans assess that great team, epitomised this work ethic.

United played many a fine game under McLean, and each fan will have his favourite. It could be the Monchengladbach demolition, running Monaco ragged, or the humbling of PSV Eindhoven on their own patch in the1982 UEFA Cup tie. But for me, the annihilation of Standard Liege in the second round of the European Cup run of 1983-84 was the best whole 90 minutes I ever saw United play.

Liege had been crowned champions of Belgium just a few months previously, but on Wednesday, November 2nd, 1983, United dismantled them in front of an attendance close on 17,000 at Tannadice.

It was a game United controlled for 90 minutes. United played a "European style" better than a European team. Jim McLean sent the team out to play to their strengths, the speed of Milne, the passing ability of Eamonn Bannon, the predatory instincts of Davie Dodds, and the aerial power of Paul Hegarty.

Right from the first whistle, the result was never in doubt, indeed it was four

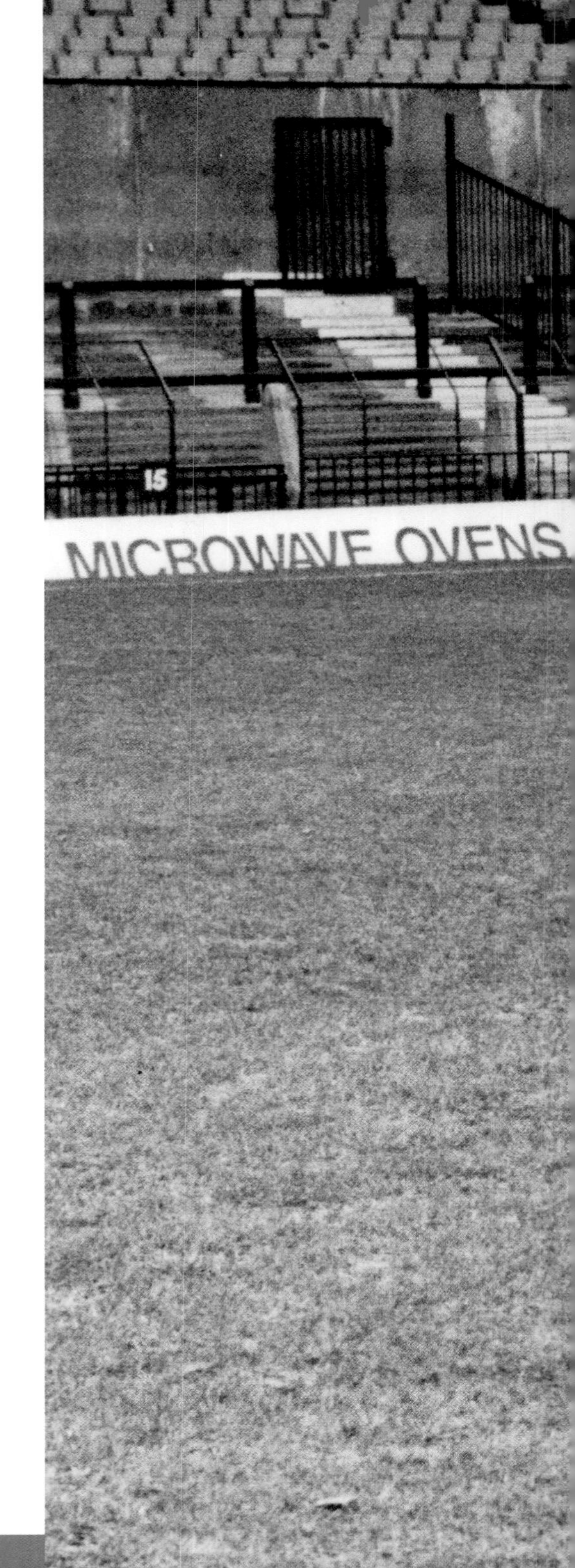

Jim taking training at Old Trafford, the night before the 1984 UEFA tie.

169
SHARP
MARTINI
MARTINI
the best GILLETTE

going on ten. Every part of the team played to the peak of its ability, it was a precision instrument.

But, more of note, this was a highly sophisticated performance. Many too many times, we fans in Scotland have looked at visiting European teams and thought that they looked assured, had a bit more savvy than our players, had a bit more know-how. Well that's how United were that evening. The lads in tangerine were the clever ones, the well-drilled unit, the experienced team rather than the naive underdogs.

It was a night that every United supporter who saw it will always remember. It was from then on that United were a different proposition in Europe.

The very next round showed how good the United European machine had become.

Jim would famously say the team had a domestic way of playing and a continental way of playing. And if you think about some of the games that were to follow, you can see exactly what he meant by that.

The games against Rapid Vienna, the opposition in that 1984 European Cup Quarter-Final, are another superb example of what Jim's coaching achieved.

The Austrians had a collection of world-class individuals in their side, including one of Austria's all-time-great goalscorers, the 69-times-capped Hans Krankl, and the incredibly fast Christian Keglevits, and also the coolest-of-the-cool Czech midfielder Antonin Panenka, who is still

Jim excelled at getting his ideas across to his team.

adidas
27
2

referenced by TV commentators every time a chipped penalty is scored.

United lost the first leg 2-1, but had the crucial away goal. Then at Tannadice a fortnight later, on March 21st, 1984, Jim's team put in a masterful in-depth defensive performance, with an amazingly high workrate, but also a very sophisticated attacking one. Davie Dodds scored the winner in the 21st minute, but from then on played almost as a defensive midfielder.

This one wasn't an exceptional attacking display, but it was very clever game management. Again, this was what commentators like to call a "very European" way of playing.

Most remarkably when you look back, though, we United supporters fully expected to beat Rapid Vienna, who were a huge club, the best in their nation by a distance – there were 38,000 Rapid fans in attendance for their home leg.

The Arab legions went to Tannadice, all 18,865 of us that night, knowing that United could take on the best that Austria had to offer and beat them.

It was tense, and it wasn't easy. Keglevits set off for a run and got off an on-target shot late in the second half that provided just about the worst heart-in-mouth moment I've ever experienced at a football match.

But United beat them. Jim had watched them, assessed them, worked out a way to play them, saw where their weaknesses were, and over the two legs got the better of them.

The following year, Jim took advantage of the lazy assumptions of Ron Atkinson to shock Manchester United at Old Trafford. The Red Devils obviously hadn't learned much from watching Dundee United because they allowed their left-sided attacker, Jesper Olsen, to track back to mark United's right-back, Richard Gough, at set-pieces. Jim had done his preparation well, Big Ron might have been a bit of a TV celebrity, but he hadn't done his homework very well.

He'd clearly only ordered the obvious thing, the normal thing – he told his players to go with their man and make sure to mark him.

But Gough's ability to head the ball far outmatched wee Jesper's ability to get to the ball before him. Every free-kick was fired at Gough, who would head back across the 18-yard area. United's first goal in the 2-2 draw came directly from that tactic.

By this point, though, United supporters had become a sophisticated bunch themselves.

All of us had become experienced in the European game. We knew how United would play, we knew what the plan was. We didn't get too impatient if things weren't quite going the team's way, we knew that Jim would work it out. It was a great time to be going to Tannadice. Missing a game was like missing a lesson in how football should be played.

Another remarkable thing we United supporters could expect to see was our players getting better every season, sometimes better every week. This was because

■ **Jim directing a Scotland training session in 1979.**

Jim worked on flaws. Indeed, he would go looking for flaws to iron out. If a player was weak with his left, then it would be worked upon. If a player thought he was specialised in one position, then Jim coached that out of him. Any United supporter who remembers David Narey playing will know that Jim would sometimes push him forward into midfield, depending on what job the team needed doing.

Billy Kirkwood was played as a man-marker, and was exceptional in that role, probably the best Dundee United player I've seen without the ball. But he was also a ball-winner and an intelligent distributor when he had won it.

Both John Clark and Paul Hegarty saw many on-pitch minutes as strikers. Paul had, indeed, been bought as a striker from Hamilton Accies in 1974.

Sometimes it was difficult to understand the role Derek Stark was playing. He was a defensive player, but popped up in the opposition box an awful lot, and he scored some telling goals. Three different people would probably point to three different places if pinpointing his position in a 4-3-3.

If it was difficult for the fans to work out, think what a nightmare it must have been for opposition players and managers. And if we supporters didn't fully understand how Jim was bamboozling the opposition, we certainly enjoyed it.

But let's have a go at trying to unravel what Jim was doing. Once he had recruited players capable of doing what was asked of them, what were these tactics he coached into them as a unit?

This might sound odd, but while it was sophisticated it wasn't complicated, and Jim has explained it many times. He had studied the West German and Dutch teams of the late 1960s and early '70s. He looked at what they did and how they did it.

And that was to make passes, keep the ball on the ground, play possession football. The aim was to work the ball forwards, sometimes at pace, and find gaps between the opposition defenders.

Now this is a blindingly easy thing to say, an obvious thing to say. But it is not an easy thing for a football team to do. If it was, then every team would do it brilliantly well. Any fan can see that not every player, or every team, can do it.

Simply put, that is what Jim got his teams to do.

Jim has another trait that again sounds almost stupidly simple, and is very easy to say, but isn't at all easy to put into practice. He listens, thinks about what is said and acts upon it.

In any interview he has ever given he will talk about people he admires in the game. Jock Stein, John Prentice, Bobby Seith, Eddie Turnbull, Johnny Low, Walter McCrae . . . it's a long list. But it is one thing to listen to great men talk, but a rare skill to analyse what they say, recognise the patterns they are describing about their own teams, and apply it to the problems a completely different set of men (his own team) had in playing a winning game.

If this sounds like statements of the blatantly obvious,

Jim and Jock at the World Cup, 1982.

then I apologise. Though while it is obvious, it is in no way a common skill to be able to do.

But Jim did it.

This coaching ability didn't go unnoticed. Jim was invited by one of these men he greatly admired, Jock Stein, to assist with the national team, a job he did for four years. But there was a surprise awaiting him when he got to his first training session with the Scotland players.

They weren't as good as he thought they'd be.

Indeed he is on record as saying he appreciated his own players a little more once his horizons had been widened by mixing with internationals. But that, in itself, is further testament to Jim's coaching ability. His United players were as good as, or better than, stars from the English First Division (as it was at that time) because he had made them better, coached them better, and educated them in the game better.

But if there is one thing, one aspect of football that truly speaks for what Jim McLean achieved as a coach then it is another plain and simple point. It is that while Dundee United had good players in Jim's heyday, the whole was greater than the sum of the parts. It was the team that was magnificent, not one of the stars in it (very, very good though many of them were).

Jim McLean's Dundee United were a team that operated well. Jim would make fine adjustments to formation, or give instructions on where he wanted attacks to start when the team had controlled possession, or place a man in an area of the pitch that would ruin the opposition's plans.

It takes a team to do that. It takes a level of organisation and repeated training sessions to do that.

Most of all, however, it takes an ability to communicate. Jim imposed his vision of how his teams would play upon the members of his team. When you hear one of his star players say, "Everyone had a job to do, and knew how to do it", you have to think, "But how did he do that".

He did it by having a clear vision of what he wanted and explaining it, demonstrating it, to players who might very well have their own egotistical ideas about how their own personal skills might best be showcased in a game. But the game of football, and the way Jim wanted it played, wasn't to benefit any individual. It was to get a team working the way he wanted it to work. And Jim knew exactly how he wanted his teams to work.

That is what all great managers do. The reason that some who have been fantastic players do not make fantastic managers is that they can't properly get their ideas across, they can't make their players do what they could do on a football field. Football is about 11 men carrying out one man's plan. The "plan" is usually referred to as "tactics" in our football slang.

In the case of Dundee United, 1971 to 1993, the man doing the planning was James McLean, football genius.

■ A United golf outing to Gleneagles in 1981. Jim created a team, not a collection of individuals.

178
THE FINEST PRESERVES IN THE WORLD
Keiller
THE FINEST CONFECTIONERY IN THE WORLD
HALIFAX BUILDING SOCIETY
CIS INSURANCE
TSB
KOLFOR PLANT
MURRAY
METALS

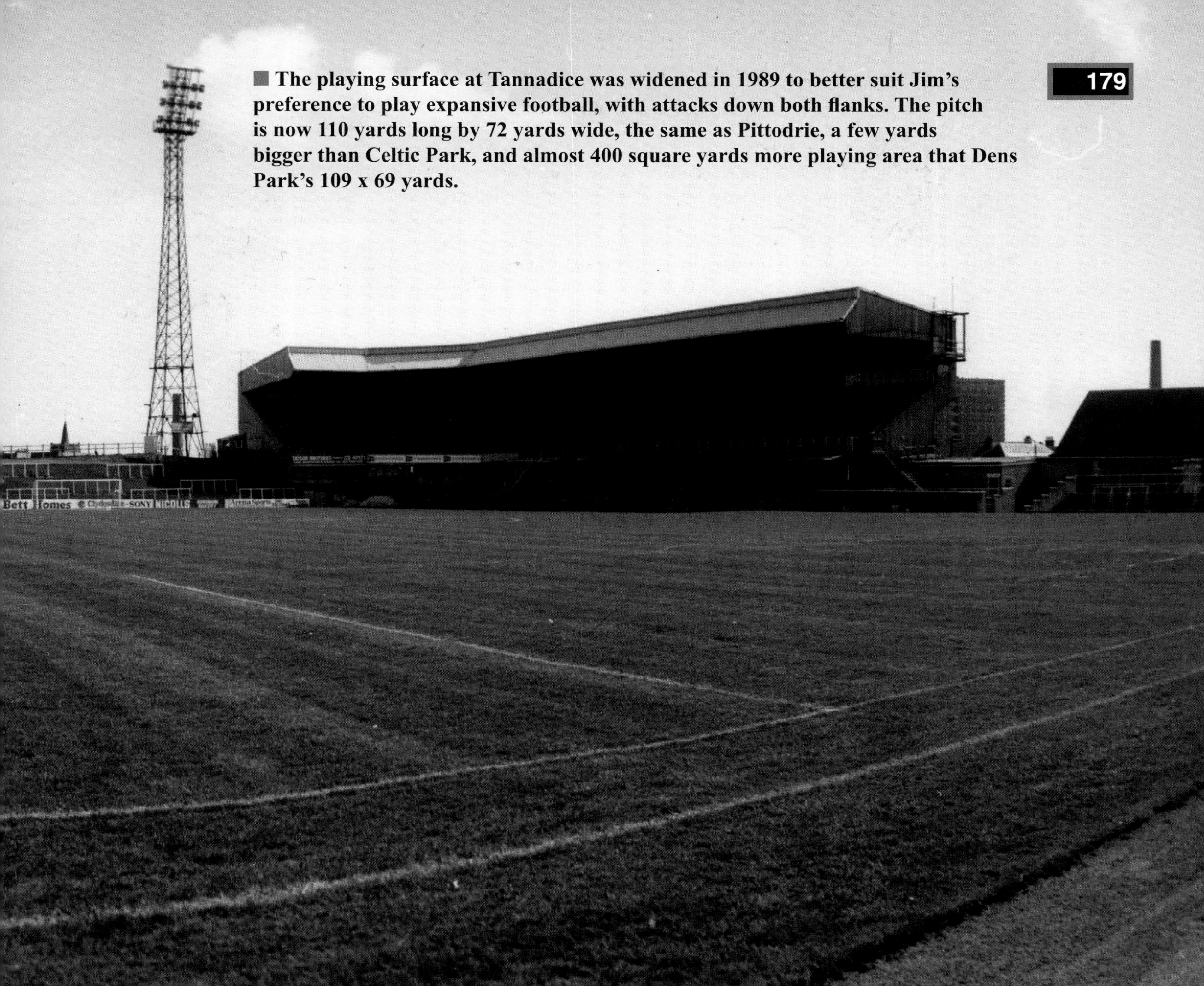

■ The playing surface at Tannadice was widened in 1989 to better suit Jim's preference to play expansive football, with attacks down both flanks. The pitch is now 110 yards long by 72 yards wide, the same as Pittodrie, a few yards bigger than Celtic Park, and almost 400 square yards more playing area that Dens Park's 109 x 69 yards.

Everyone got a selection box and £10

FAN TRIBUTE: SIMON ADAMSON, COALTOWN OF BALGONIE.

I HAVE many good memories of Jim McLean. As a disabled supporter I must pay tribute to Jim for how kind he and Doris were towards us all in his time as manager.

Every Christmas for most of the '80s he would gift each disabled supporter with a selection box along with a card with £10 inside.

Those were the days when £10 would get you a ticket for a match v. Barcelona!

I also had the opportunity to sit next to the home dugout until the disabled area moved (Hah, I think he got annoyed at us telling him his tactics weren't working!)

It was amazing to see him in action, motivating players to reach their full potential.

Jim gave me some of the best memories of my 40 years as an Arab. I only wish I was older to appreciate fully what his teams achieved, as we took it all for granted at the time.

FAN TRIBUTE: IAIN TAYLOR.

IN the late '80s my dad (a fanatical Arab) became house-bound.

But he regularly wrote to Jim, offering praise, talking tactics, giving criticism or just banter.

Every letter, Jim answered personally. This was amazing.

At Christmas he sent my parents wine, which was delivered by two United players. This, to me, sums the great man up.

FAN TRIBUTE: STEVE GROSSI.

JIM took on the best coaches in Europe and left them standing.

My memories are of his tactics and the way his teams attacked.

The players and performances he gave us will live in my memory for ever. His unbelievable achievements will never, ever be matched.

Incredible coach. Never given the credit he deserved. Great memories.

FAN TRIBUTE: FRASER LOGAN.

WHEN I look back at those magical Jim McLean years, I realise I went to every game with the expectation of winning.

We didn't think then that we might not see this type of constant success for a long time, or maybe even never again.

Jim was a tactical genius, working with a small squad of players, unlike the masses we see these days.

The European nights under the floodlights always had a magical atmosphere.

In December 1992 my son Craig was the mascot for a United-Aberdeen league game. It was a great day for us all, we met both Doris and Jim. After the warm-up we were sitting in the dressing room as the players drifted back in.

When they came in the door Jim would say to each of them "You are NOT Craig's favourite player!" until Jim McInally came in to Jim saying, "You ARE Craig's favourite player!" It was hilarious.

The banter in the dressing room was electric. Jim was giving everyone pelters about how bad they'd been in the last match and what he expected from them this time.

The final result was a 2-2 draw, after United being two goals down.

Despite his gruff exterior persona he couldn't have been nicer or more accommodating and this was right before the kick-off of a big game.

FAN TRIBUTE: ROY MATTHEWS.

I WAS a founder member and secretary of the Dundee United Business Club and during that time I enjoyed long and fascinating chats with Jim over a cup of tea in his office. I also received tickets for the directors' boxes at various grounds for midweek games when my work took me to Glasgow.

The memory that sticks most is the occasion when my key broke in the lock of my car after a cup semi-final on a Wednesday night in Glasgow.

My daughter and I were stranded. But when Jim heard of our plight he insisted that we come back with him on the team bus to Tannadice. He then arranged a taxi to take us back to our Monikie home. A typical act of generosity from a remarkable man.

FAN TRIBUTE: EVAN McDONALD.

FOR a couple of seasons in the '70s I sold match day programmes and met Doris and Mrs Lindsay, who counted the money and were always really nice.

One game, against Celtic, I was walking out of the tunnel, just having cashed up. I was wearing my United scarf and tammy. I went to go round the track towards the north terracing, but Jim McLean caught me and said, "They'll eat you alive if you walk in front of them dressed like that. Go round the other way, son."

I was proud that he was looking out for me like that.

Oor Jim was as hard as nails

FAN TRIBUTE: J. McLEOD.

I WAS invited to Ibrox for a United game, during the 1988-89 season I think (I lose track of all the seasons!) I was with my wife, as a corporate guest of a large banking organisation, and we were seated in the posh part of the main stand.

Posh or not, one of the Rangers supporters, who looked quite civilised in suit and tie and camel coat, must have had too many sarsaparillas because he got a bit carried away.

Maurice Malpas was playing a blinder, I think he might have been deployed in central defence that day, and he was anticipating everything the Rangers forwards tried. What a player Mo was.

The well-dressed chap stood up, leaned over the seats in front, and shouted (phlegm flying) "Break that b****** Malpas's f****** legs".

We hadn't even noticed that Jim McLean was sitting a few rows behind us, he must have been serving a touchline ban and had arrived late in his seat.

But he got up, crossed the gangway stairs, and got right into the shouter's face, his finger jabbing. He took the bloke to the cleaners, loudly saying that this was a man's career, his livelihood, his health, that he was shouting about.

Jim left him without a name, and all the people around us were hushed by this display of righteous anger.

The bloke – and he was a big fellah – tried to argue, but Jim, who used industrial language himself I have to say, completely shut him down.

Eventually a steward, then it grew to be three stewards, stepped in to (we thought) eject the man who had been shouting – though I think he was merely moved to another seat.

But Jim was absolutely right. The bloke was an obnoxious, drunken moron. Any true Rangers fan would have been ashamed – and in fact not one person around him attempted to defend him.

We were incredibly impressed by Jim's bravery to confront that idiot in the middle of a stand full of opposition supporters.

My wife still talks about it to this day, whenever Jim McLean is mentioned.

Jim didn't give it a thought. He called it out exactly as he saw it. He told that bloke his opinion of him.

Jim McLean is, and always will be, a Dundee United hero.

■ Jim grew up in Lanarkshire, playing football and working on building sites. Drunks in camel coats would be unlikely to intimidate him.

We gave our jobs the very best we had

TRIBUTE: MRS ELLA LINDSAY.

MRS ELLA LINDSAY started at Dundee United in 1969 and became Scottish football's first-ever female club secretary in 1972. She remained in that post, performing admirably, until retiring in 1985.

She is still as sharp as a tack today. When that "sharp as a tack" idiom is used, it is often followed by a qualifier such as "for a woman of 90". But Mrs Lindsay (as everyone at Tannadice called her) is an intelligent, capable and eloquent woman. She uses a stick to help her get around these days but there is no sign of her brain ageing. She doesn't look or sound anything like 90.

Like Doris McLean, she assesses me, conducts a short interrogation on what manner, exactly, of book I am working on? Who is it aimed at? What am I trying to prove with it? Only when satisfied with my answers does she give me a smile.

When she does start talking about the past, she gives me an insightful breakdown into the changes the Bosman Ruling had on the game in Scotland, including a withering assessment of Mr Bosman's footballing abilities. She listens to my bumbling opinions in return (it must have been quickly apparent that I was much less aware of Jean-Marc's playing career than she was… my pretence of knowing, oh yeah – of course, he was capped for Belgium U-21s doesn't fool her for a second.)

But I pass the worth-speaking-to test. I think. I had a bit of a smooth-the-way advantage, as I know one of her sons, and she opens up her store of Tannadice memories to me.

In the male-dominated world of football, it took a strong woman to break the mould and reach the position Mrs Lindsay reached. She had experience of running a sports organisation from working at Dundee Ice Rink – and was once Scotland's ice dance champion. So she knew about the particular demands of a sports administration environment and was prepared when the United directors put her in charge of the daily functioning of the behind-the-scenes part of the club.

No one needs me to point out how much work that would have entailed. Getting a team to Bremen, Eindhoven, or even Kilmarnock, on time, with all their kit, and without stresses to distract them from playing at the peak of their powers, isn't a simple thing.

She obviously excelled at this. She worked on a daily basis with Doris who was often at Tannadice and heavily involved in organising and operating the place on match days. Ella did everything, all the unique and sometimes

■ Club captain Paul Hegarty, Mrs Lindsay, chairman Johnston Grant and Jim McLean with the 1979 Scottish League Cup.

downright strange things that are needed to run a top-flight football club.

And for almost 15 years she worked every day with Jim McLean. So what was he like to work with?

"He was always a gentleman towards me," says Mrs Lindsay "I heard him get angry at other people, the players or sometimes referees, if that's what you are asking. But he was unfailingly polite to other members of staff. I thoroughly enjoyed working with him.

"He worked incredibly hard. Put in long hours every single day.

"And he did lots of things that were never seen.

"People would write to him. Not just United supporters, although a lot of them did. But people who ran their own football teams, Sunday boys teams, or amateur teams.

"There were a lot of letters asking for advice, asking about tactics and training methods and how to go about getting the best out of players. Jim answered every one of them. Sometimes he would meet the people who had written in. And I don't think I've ever read reports in the papers of him doing that. Though there were lots of letters thanking him for it.

"He was a great one for the grass roots of football. And was the first person I ever heard use that 'grass roots' phrase. But he was aware of how important it was that football operated well at all levels. And he knew that if he had a connection with the game at the kids' level, when these teams had a good player they would remember who had been helpful to them. And they would recommend the best players came to Tannadice and know that their players would do well if they got the attention of Jim McLean.

"And he made things happen that the supporters didn't ever know about. He had an effect on the whole place. Everyone at Tannadice back then had a pride about what they did and how they did it. Everyone felt that they had to do their job to Jim McLean's standards, the cleaners, the groundsmen, everyone. They all did their jobs to the very best of their abilities. And the coaches and scouts and players too, of course."

She says she feels sorry for United supporters who are too young to have seen United play in the 1980s. "Jim sent the team out to win games," she says. "I sometimes heard him give his instructions. His teams attacked the other lot, and found ways to beat them. There is too much side-to-side stuff nowadays, too much passing the ball backwards. You don't score goals by doing that. Jim's teams scored goals and were told to entertain the fans."

Mrs Lindsay treated the players like family, which helped grow team spirit too.

"A lot of them were just laddies away from home. They needed looking after. I remember Billy Kirkwood, when corduroy trousers were in fashion, coming and asking Evelyn Fiddes (Evelyn worked alongside Ella for many years) and me how to get the fluff off them. We did it with Sellotape. Or Ray Stewart coming up to the office just looking for a tissue to blow his nose.

"And Jim looked at what sort of boys they were

■ **Doris McLean, Ella Lindsay and Mrs Johnston Grant at the Olympic Stadium in Rome, for the European Cup semi-final 1984. The AS Roma officials did everything they could to intimidate and upset the entire United party. They gave the three ladies tickets 48, 49 and 50, allocated by name. But then discovered they had sat in seats 49, 50, and 48, and moved in aggressively to insist that each woman sat in precisely the seat allocated to her.**

before he signed them. He looked at their family to see if they would be the type who could keep his feet on the ground. They were all nice lads. They gave me some wonderful gifts when I retired and I still get lots of cards every Christmas.

"They all have grandchildren themselves now, of course. I don't know where the time went.

"Jim wouldn't have liked dealing with the agents they all have nowadays, though. He had no time for these sort of people. They aren't football people, you know. They don't want to talk about football. They are just money people. Jim would talk about football, he'd make the laddies better footballers. That was much more important."

The stories of what happened in her workplace, and the characters there, are just like stories of what happened in every office environment. Except her work involved sorting out the fans' allocation of Old Trafford tickets, or making sure John Holt and Derek Stark knew the travel arrangements for Monaco.

"Oh Princess Grace was lovely, though," this reminds Mrs Lindsay. "She was very polite, very nice manners when she came here. She spoke to everyone. Most of the people who came were nice, the other clubs' directors and managers. You treat people how you find them.

"Alex Ferguson was always very funny, he always had a joke."

She relates a story, although once she has finished it tells me that I really shouldn't put such a thing in a respectable book. But I'm going to defy her (I'm feeling brave.) She relates the tale of "some druggie" wandering in off the street and up to the Tannadice office. No security in those days.

"He wasn't dangerous at all, he was just a nuisance, a daftie. I don't think he knew where he was or what he was talking about. But he just wouldn't go away, wouldn't stop talking."

Mrs Lindsay did her best to get him out of the building, but eventually had to call upon big, bold Walter Smith to persuade him the last few steps out of the door. After the druggie had gone, she asked Walter what he had said to finally get rid of him. Wattie said, "Oh I sent him up to Dens Park!"

She also relates a tale that illustrates the relationship Jim had with Alex Ferguson.

One day, Alex phoned, looking for Jim, but he was out at training. So Mrs Lindsay took a message. It was that Aberdeen had been trying to sign a boy who was a real prospect at that time, a striker called Craig Lyon, but he was from the west and very young, so his mother didn't want him based away up in Aberdeen.

Alex generously passed on the lad's contact details, suggesting that perhaps Jim could persuade the mother to let him to sign for a club not quite such a distance from home. Better than letting him go to Celtic or Rangers, after all.

Jim duly took the number and got on the phone.

Now you'll be way ahead of me here, and way ahead of Jim too. The date was April 1st and Fergie had manoeuvred Jim into making a call to Calderpark Zoo, asking to speak to Mrs Lion!

Mrs Lindsay loves this story, and starts straight into

Ella with Alex Ferguson at Tannadice, having *almost* forgiven him for the "Craig Lyon incident".

another about Ally MacLeod, when manager of Ayr United, attempting to demonstrate exactly how his centre-half should have cleared the ball, swung his foot so hard that his shoe came off and out the dressing room door.

Doing interviews for this book was quite an experience.

Speaking to Doris McLean was like talking to royalty, she is a genuinely kind and nice person. Speaking to Allan Preston gave me a better understanding of how professional footballers think. Speaking to Sally Reid opened my eyes about how forceful characters can be presented on a stage. Allan Herriot was a very impressive and talented chap, and Phil Differ had me in stitches.

Speaking to Ella Lindsay was like talking to your favourite grandmother, and a high-functioning chief executive, all rolled into one.

She has a laser-sharp memory for detail, and she's an insightful and clever woman who deeply understood the people she worked with.

Listening to her talk brings the Dundee United of the Jim McLean era to life. She retains a great deal of respect for Mr Mclean and clearly loved, and remains very proud of, the Dundee United of her era. It is very touching.

I took it to be a measure of the working culture that was created at Tannadice Park.

A well-functioning operation, be it a window-cleaning business or a football club, works well in every nook and cranny when every member of staff is operating to the very best of their ability.

It is the manager that sets the tone and the standards to make that happen. On the park, in the admin office, cleaning the toilets – it doesn't matter what you do, you do the job right. Do the very best, the absolute best you are capable of, and do that every single day of every year.

That's what Jim McLean did at Tannadice. Those are the standards he set for everyone, from top to bottom of the organisation. It is the art of good management, and rarely achieved at a football club or in any workplace.

To illustrate what happens when this is all in place, I want to finish by telling you how Mrs Lindsay sums up the Jim McLean years at Tannadice.

This is what it all boiled down to, she reckons:

"Whether we thought Jim was watching or not, we all did the best we possibly could. Because sooner or later he actually would be looking to see what sort of job you were doing.

"And it was wonderful, all around the place, when the team won. We all wanted them to win. Everyone at Tannadice. Every game, every season, all the time. So we did our jobs the very best we were capable of, because we believed that we could help wins happen.

"Jim made us feel that way."

You're right, Mrs Lindsay. A man can do good things, but a great man can inspire a whole team.

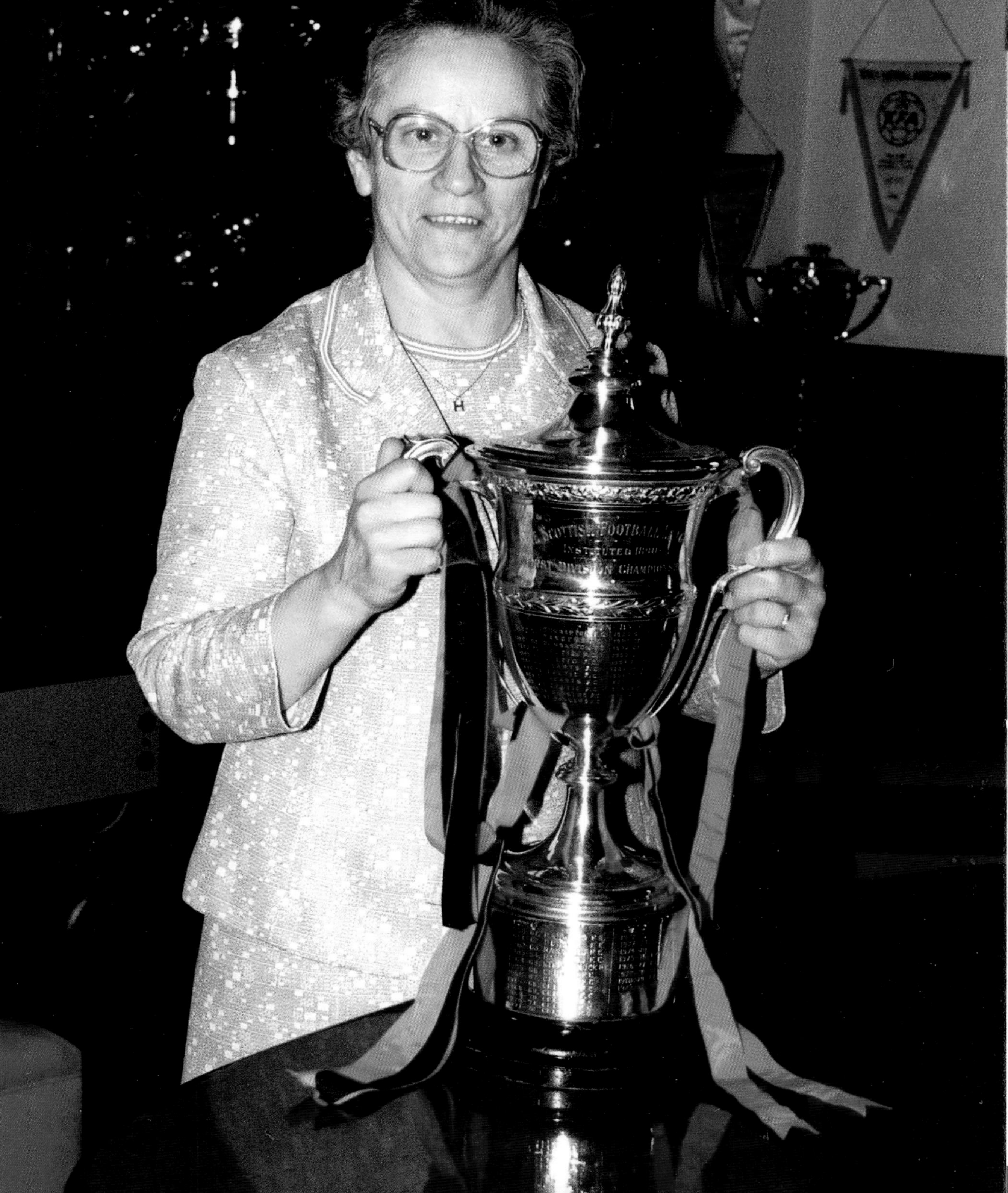

■ **This is what it was all for. Mrs Lindsay in the Dundee United boardroom, with the 1983 Scottish League Championship trophy. They had all played a part in winning it. All the staff. Everyone at Tannadice made it happen.**

A working-class man of the people

TRIBUTE: KAREN OGILVIE, LONDON.

IN the '90s I was assistant manager at the shop at Tannadice, with Jennifer Milton, and have very happy memories of those days.

We saw Jim McLean a lot and he was a complete gentleman. I thought he was always misunderstood and described unfairly in the Press.

I was just a young girl, but every time he saw me, he'd say, "Oi, where's my cuppa?" And I'd cheekily say, "It's still in the kettle, waiting for you to make it". And he always laughed, he said it to me every time. He had no airs about him, he spoke to everyone the same. We thought the world of him.

One time, I had to take a supply of balls over to the shop under the George Fox Stand and the goal nets were still up. So, being a United fan, I got a ball out and "scored" a few goals at Tannadice. I gave myself a cheer and saluted the (not there) crowd.

But then I heard a loud banging. It was Jim in his office pointing his finger at me. I could see the words he was mouthing, they were: "Get the f*** off the f****** pitch" (you know what he was like for protecting the playing surface). I thought I'd be in big trouble, but he never mentioned it again. Once he'd said his piece, he forgot about it and was just the same as always.

I really respected him for that. Although I reckon I should have been picked for the team, I'd scored a couple of good goals!

Before that, in the '80s, my dad (who was a BT engineer) went to fix a phones problem in Jim's office. Jim was there, talking to Walter Smith. But as soon as my dad came to the door Jim said, "Right Walter, out you go. Here's a man who's a REAL worker with a REAL job to do. Get yourself out of his way."

My dad reckoned Jim had lots of respect for working men. He treated everyone right. With respect. He was a man of the people.

The best story is that, at Christmas, Jim would make the players serve up Christmas dinner to the cleaners, Rose and Ann, to say thank you for their work over the year. He cared about ordinary people. He made us all feel special and we were proud to work for him.

When Jennifer and I handed in our notice, he came over personally and asked us to stay. I didn't stay, I was going to a better-paid job with more prospects. But he completely understood, he was lovely about it, and I was really touched that he'd come to speak to us.

Even when we couldn't be persuaded to stay on, he thanked us genuinely and from the heart for all our good work. I couldn't imagine a better boss.

He deserves to be recognised with a statue. He was so loyal to United, he gave his life to the club. He was one of the nicest, most down-to-earth men I ever met.

■ Jim was always protective of the playing surface, especially when assistant shop managers had been running about on it! (Pic courtesy of Dave Martin, Fotopress)

My Dad versus Jim McLean!

FAN TRIBUTE: IAIN McGARRY.

IN 1994 I was 14, rocking a "curtains" hairstyle and owning at least one fluorescent shell suit. United had just made it to our seventh Scottish Cup Final. It seemed the whole United support had sniffed Ivan Golac's flowers and were on a high. This HAD to be our year, I HAD to be there.

I'd been going to see United with my Dad since 1990 and nothing could match going to Tannadice and watching Wee Jim going mental at the linesman, the referee, every United player and I'm pretty sure Eamonn Bannon, even though he left in '88.

Tickets for the final were at a premium, and I had to hold out for the general sales. I should have known something was awry when we were told tickets would go on sale at 9 am on a midweek morning at the new George Fox stand, not the usual ticket office. But I stood in the queue with a few hundred fellow Arabs, and my Dad, from 6 am. Waiting, hoping. 9 am came, 9:10 . . . 9:20. Nothing.

Then someone from the main ticket office turned up and said there were no tickets left.

I learned a few new swear words from my usually placid Dad. He was raging, and for the one and only time that I ever saw he was spoiling for a fight. Dad went

■ **Iain's hard-won, but "restricted view" Cup Final tickets.**

racing to the ticket office looking for any staff member, but all we saw was Jim McLean getting out of his car.

The next few minutes are a blur, I remember my Dad going right up to Jim, nose-to-nose, and giving him the hairdryer treatment. My Dad was doing a wee Jim on wee Jim! I was mortified.

But during all the conflict all I can remember was thinking it was odd that my Dad was going pure mental but still had the civility to call him "Mr McLean".

I was ready for Jim's reaction. Surely he wouldn't take this abuse. Jim remained calm and said to wait. A few minutes later he came back out the Tannadice door and apologised to the growing crowd, saying there had been a miscommunication. But there were only restricted-view tickets for the first few rows at Hampden.

He'd been going to send them back because he reckoned they were unsellable. However, he would put them back on sale. We got the tickets! Front row near the corner flag. We still paid full price, no way was wee Jim taking a total loss that day. But my dad won! And so did United in the final.

My Dad passed away from cancer a few years before the 2010 Scottish Cup victory. While that was a magic day, nothing compares to 1994, sitting next to my Dad, my real hero, hugging each other at the final whistle with tears in our eyes.

Thank you champ, and thank you Mr McLean.

FAN TRIBUTE: GORDON HAY.

NOT a football-related story but one that sums up Jim's sharp wit.

A few years ago I was the community policeman in Broughty Ferry. One day I was in Brook Street and accidentally walked into a ladies' boutique.

Quickly I realised my mistake and about-turned into the street – only to be met by Jim and Doris.

As quick as a flash Jim said, "You'll no get anything to fit you in there, son."

FAN TRIBUTE: DAVE HART.

I WAS fortunate, as a fan for more than 50 years, to get to know Jim very well.

I met him through playing five-a-sides with United backroom staff every Friday (30 years ago). I then frequently played golf with him at Downfield where we were members.

Once he trusted you he was a very warm and open person.

He was my hero for what he brought to United. I would hang on every word, his knowledge of football and thoughts on players were fantastic.

He once told me they had a skinny, 15-year-old centre-forward and I should watch him in a game at Gardyne College pitch. The young lad was Duncan Ferguson.

The next week Jim asked what I thought, and I said my bit. He then talked for about an hour on what he saw in him, what he would work on to improve, and how good Dunc could be.

It was brilliant. The rest is history.

I don't think any book or TV programme can properly capture this legend of a football man and person. I hope your book can go some way towards putting into words how brilliant he was as a manager.

People need to know the persona portrayed in the media is only one side. He was also warm, witty and the most interesting person I've ever spoken to. Something that few people, I suppose, ever saw.

The man who gave United Dignity

TRIBUTE: DEACON BLUE ROCK STAR AND DJ RICKY ROSS.

I HAD just started secondary school when Jim McLean arrived at Tannadice in 1971.

I was part of a stupid mob who had chanted "Kerr must go" at the previous manager, too ignorant of his towering achievements and bored by the mundanity of survival.

I'd seen McLean play in 1970's Scottish Cup semi-final between Kilmarnock and Aberdeen at Muirton.

I then became aware of the impact he made at Dundee. Every other Saturday my Dad and I went to Dens. So we knew what he could do, the effect he had had on that team. We were delighted at this new, young, track-suited boss.

In the years that followed Jim McLean made steady but, by today's standards, barely discernible progress.

In those days relegation wasn't a very real possibility as we were in a league of 18 teams. When the Premier League started we narrowly avoided the drop which took Dundee down and started their 20-year downward spiral.

It was ironic, then, that in the early years of the Premier League, which Jim McLean openly opposed, United started to make some ground. I remember the young players starting to arrive: Payne, Narey, Holt. Andy Gray and Raymond Stewart. Stewart and Gray were sold, but Holt and Narey stayed to be joined by the likes of Sturrock, Milne and Malpas.

Sexy football? I remember a frisson of excitement as I passed them all running along the Kingsway one day during the summer holidays; McLean leading from the front sporting an old woollen tammy which covered the dwindling strands of hair.

Success didn't come overnight. But remarkably it didn't disappear immediately either.

The story of Dundee's 1962 league win had been overshadowed in the town's football lore by the unseemly haste with which the star players of the team had been dispatched after the triumph. Ure, Gilzean, Cook all went south and the team never achieved that success again apart from a brief flurry in the early seventies when (aided by Jim McLean) they'd built a side capable of winning the League Cup. United's League Cup triumph in '79 was only a start.

It led to McLean retaining the trophy the following year and reaching the final of the Scottish Cup in '81.

But the real deal was still to come. Between 1983 and 1987 United were to do what no Scottish club outside the Old Firm (and let's be honest we can include them too!) will ever achieve again.

They won the league, reached two more Scottish Cup Finals, the semi-final of the European Cup (when it only accepted real champions!) and the final of the UEFA Cup.

No football supporter has a right to expect any of that. Not only did we do all that but no players were transferred from the club and the squad continued to be strengthened from the flow of young players joining at schoolboy level.

I say all this for one reason. To pay respect to the man who made us so happy: Jim McLean.

This was someone who achieved all of the above. And when the "ultimate" Scottish job was offered, Rangers, he refused to go. There were people moaning then. There were journalists telling us how grumpy he was and how badly the players were treated even in these days. It always struck me as odd that no one seemed to care about the lot of run-of-the-mill players playing in mediocre teams, but the Scottish media (all Glasgow based) perceived McLean's empire at Tannadice to be a real threat to the accepted norms.

That is why it is wrong to imagine that some unfortunate BBC journalist who was just in the wrong place at the wrong time should ever be caught up in Jim's story.

I feel sorry for John Barnes. He had done nothing wrong but became synonymous with the downfall of a legend. I'm sure he wishes it were otherwise.

But the Jim McLean story is too mighty to be

■ **United fans regularly sing the anthem *Dignity* in tribute to the team, and to Ricky and Deacon Blue.**

overshadowed by that one incident. In my opinion he is on a par with Jock Stein, and Alex Ferguson in building truly great all-time Scottish XIs the likes of which will probably never be seen again. Yes the players may have called him "Wee Jim" but they knew and we now know he is a colossus of Scottish Football.

When I first got a chance to travel to Spain, Germany and Italy I loved talking football with journalists and radio people I met.

When they asked me which team I supported (unlike their English counterparts) they all knew Dundee United.

No wonder. United had beaten the Italian champions Roma, they'd wiped out Barcelona and disposed of Werder Bremen and Borussia Monchengladbach.

I felt justifiably proud that Jim McLean's team had put my home town on the map.

I never met him until around 1989 when I was involved with Paul Sturrock's testimonial season. Since that first time he was never anything other than polite and kind to me and my family.

He welcomed us to games and always made a point of seeing me when I visited the ground.

Everyone referred to him as "The Boss".

There have been a few people worthy of that name: My Dad, Springsteen, and a few you might want to add.

But lest it be left unsaid: for we happy few who had a chance to be there when everything came good, Jim McLean was, and in my book will always be, The Boss.

Mr McLean (I could never call you by your first name) I can't thank you enough for all the happy memories.

The Boss in action.

How Elaine saved Billy Thomson!

FAN TRIBUTE: ELAINE LINTON, BROUGHTY FERRY.

IN the ’80s, in my early teen years, after every game I hung around outside the Tannadice players’ entrance to get autographs.

On one occasion I asked Jim for his autograph. I said “Mr McLean, can you please sign my book, make it to Elaine”. He said, “You’ll have to spell that out lass, I’ve got all boys, I don’t know how to spell girls’ names.”

Then, in 1989 Billy Thomson was reported to be leaving United but it wasn’t confirmed. I wrote a letter pleading with Jim to please not sell my favourite player. He wrote back, gently explaining he wanted to keep Billy but it was all about contracts.

Two weeks later, there was a headline on the back of the Evening Tele saying: THOMSON RE-SIGNS. “Oh my God”, I squealed.

I like to think that it was my input that saved Billy!

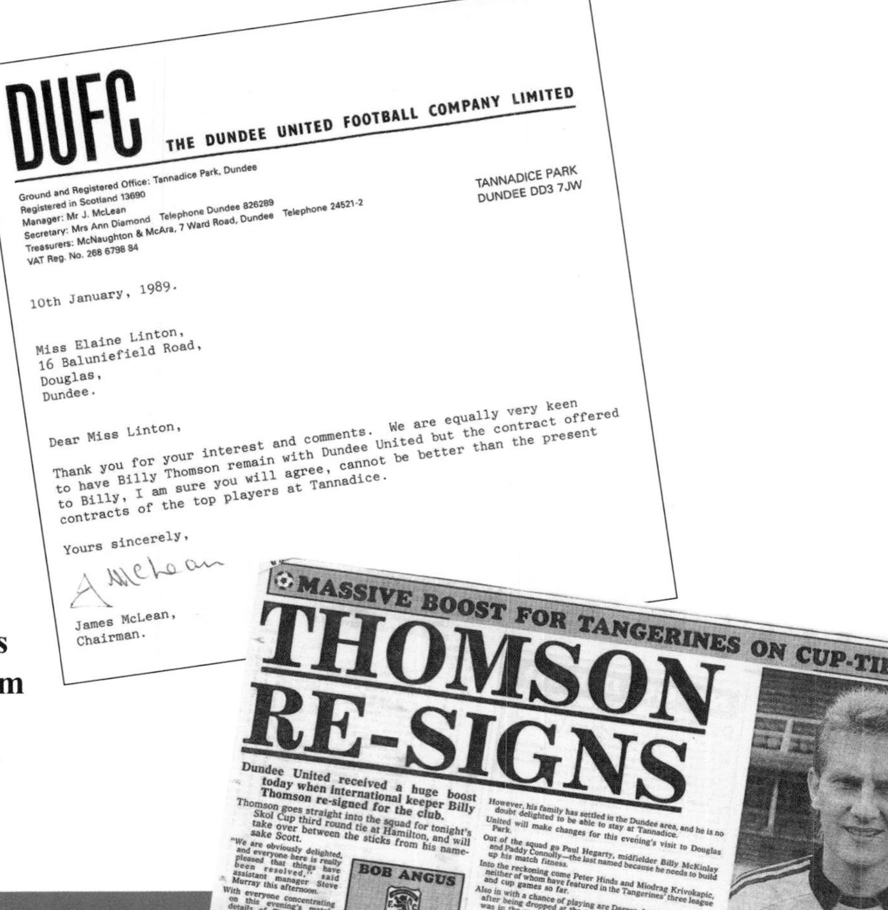

DUFC THE DUNDEE UNITED FOOTBALL COMPANY LIMITED

Ground and Registered Office: Tannadice Park, Dundee
Registered in Scotland 13690
Manager: Mr J. McLean
Secretary: Mrs Ann Diamond Telephone Dundee 826289
Treasurers: McNaughton & McAra, 7 Ward Road, Dundee Telephone 24521-2
VAT Reg. No. 268 6798 84

TANNADICE PARK
DUNDEE DD3 7JW

10th January, 1989.

Miss Elaine Linton,
16 Baluniefield Road,
Douglas,
Dundee.

Dear Miss Linton,

Thank you for your interest and comments. We are equally very keen to have Billy Thomson remain with Dundee United but the contract offered to Billy, I am sure you will agree, cannot be better than the present contracts of the top players at Tannadice.

Yours sincerely,

J McLean

James McLean,
Chairman.

MASSIVE BOOST FOR TANGERINES ON CUP-TIE

THOMSON RE-SIGNS

Dundee United received a huge boost today when international keeper Billy Thomson re-signed for the club.

Thomson goes straight into the squad for tonight's Skol Cup third round tie at Hamilton, and will take over between the sticks from his namesake Scott.

"We are obviously delighted, and everyone here is really pleased that things have been resolved," said assistant manager Steve Murray this afternoon.

With everyone concentrating on this evening's match, details of Thomson's new contract were not being released, although

BOB ANGUS

However, his family has settled in the Dundee area, and he is no doubt delighted to be able to stay at Tannadice.

United will make changes for this evening's visit to Douglas Park.

Out of the squad go Paul Hegarty, midfielder Billy McKinlay and Paddy Connolly—the last named because he needs to build up his match fitness.

Into the reckoning come Peter Hinds and Miodrag Krivokapic, neither of whom have featured in the Tangerines' three league and cup games so far.

Also in with a chance of playing are Darren Jackson, returning after being dropped at the weekend, and Charlie Adam, who was in the squad for the derby but not required

Left: Elaine’s photo with Jim after getting his autograph. Right: Elaine’s 1991 letter from Jim, and the squeal-worthy Tele headline.

FAN TRIBUTE: IAIN TAYLOR.

JIM, thanks for all the fantastic memories you gave everyone who supports United.

On a personal note, I remember in the '70s as a teenager going to Tannadice to collect a Scotland v. England ticket.

I fully expected to see a secretary, but behind the desk was Jim McLean. He said, "If eh find oot you sell this on the black market, you will never have anither season ticket at Tannadice."

Added to that was a stare I have never forgotten.

Total respect.

FAN TRIBUTE: GRAHAM BYRNE.

JIM brought many years of good memories for the club and fans. I had the pleasure of joining him for a pre-match meal, along with the players, on a visit to Parkhead back in 1978.

Jim made sure I was spoiled that day (although we lost to Celtic). I was just a young teen but he took the time to chat and calm my nerves. He even made sure the bus dropped me off right at my door.

I can't wait to see the unveiling of his well-deserved statue.

Thanks for the great times, Jim McLean.

FAN TRIBUTE: BRIAN PATON.

WHEN I was at Menzieshill High School, me and a pal wrote to Tannadice, asking to go in and take some pictures.

This would have been around 1984, I'd have been 14 at the time. United invited us in.

We tried Dundee as well but they never replied.

United gave us access to the changing rooms while Luggy, John Clark, Eamonn Bannon and all the great stars were in there.

Then we spotted Jim McLean. I was a bit scared, but asked if I could get a photo of him. He couldn't have been nicer. He took us to the pitch beside the dugout, took some photos and had a wee chat.

It's something I'll remember for the rest of my life.

FAN TRIBUTE: STEWART MacKAY.

I HAD the pleasure to be in Jim's office prior to a United match about 25 years ago. A nicer man you could not meet. For more than half an hour he told many football stories that had me sitting on the edge of my seat. It was a never-to-be-forgotten occasion for a lifelong Arab.

He is one of the kindest people I have ever met. Thanks for the memories, Sir Jim.

Wee Jim

A poyum by Dundee's street poet, Gary Robertson

L-E-H-J-I-N-D
Thatz how itz sade an spelt in oor hame toon Dundee
An thirz no minny earn that title, thirz no minny mak the grade
Sum mibbee hink thir lehjindz — the shine at furst then fade
Well back in 1971, wen Johnnie Reggae wiz in the chartz
The real deal arrehved at Tannadice, a new era wiz aboot ti start
A man as hard as Desprit Dan, ee wiz tough an fit an lean
Step aside Bruce Lee — git oot the weh, Enter The Dragon — Jim McLean

Wi a torso like Geordie Kidd's, an a brullyint futba bren
Ee trained they boyz like Spartanz, showed thum how ti play like men
Christ, ee hud thum swaggerin aboot, strollin doon the Ferry beach
The wir kickin sand in abdeez pussiz, showin the wifies thir new physiques

Regularz like Rolland, Copland an Smith, an Tommy Traynor ti name a few
Wir jined beh Knox, Kopel an Fleming, an ithirz thit Jim brought throo
An ee gave the laddies thir chance, a youth policy second ti none
Jim's vision wiz a masterstroke, an wid pye off in yearz ti come

Progress wiz stiddee an sure, but wahr the f*** wir ah the fanz?
Nae doot shoppin at Jimmy Reid's, pannin windeez in or visitin thir granz
Jim's entrepreneurial side shone throo, an ee set ti pit mettirz right
Organezzed half-time peh-eatin contests, an fir the mair boisterous — puhlly fights
Well the Shimmy took up the latter, but puhllayz wir naewahr ti be seen
Mair like 10-hole Doc Mehrtin baitz, fir the Perth Pak an the Aiberdeen!
Jim's tangerine locomotive wiz now rollin, success wizna that far aff
Ah helped beh eez infimiss pep-talks — bouncin up an doon an goin f***in daft!

Scottish Cup finalists in 1974, an ivree year creepin up the league
Mind, a wee scare in 1976, nae wurries tho — itz Dundee wah wir seeck
Then finally, League Cup success in 1979, an follyed up again in 1980
Wut a skwaad — McAlpine, Doadzee, Luggy, Wullie Pettigrew, Heggie, Holty, Narey
Then the cat got the cream, a tangerine dream — Premier League Champs in 83
Ah the sweeter fir Jim as ee lissind ti the din, thid won it at Dens Park Dundee!
Ach, the Scottish Cup aye remained elusive, an ee nearly lifted twa Euro cups
Nivir mind, fae Barca ti Borussia, humpt thum ah — an we ah lapped it up

Now, abdee kenz Jimbo's hard as nailz, but some wir plehn ignorant ti the fact
John Barnes an a certain playirz Old Man, learned the hard weh an got thir pussiz cracked!
An that famous Wullie Miller semi, wen Heggie got sent aff at Dens
Wullie didna half sh*** eez shoartz tho, wen Jim lost the plot an lit uhm ken
An eez ane playirz nivir escaped the wrath, especially that day at Motherwell
6-1? No entertainin inuff!" Ee fined thum ah an gave thum f***in hell!
Big Dunc, Big Clarky, Davie Bowman, ee tamed thum ah at Boot Camp McLean
OK — so ee wiz a greetin pus, but ee gave wi teamz the best wiv ivir seen

Now, eh started lehjind so ehl feenish, nae sh*** Jim — thatz wut ye are
Fae sma provincial ti ane o Europe's best, ye showed thum ah United's boyz kid spar
Ye went toe-ti-toe in Hellz Arena, on turf near an far ye took the lot
Ye fed yir teamz wi self-belief — Opposition? Ye cared nut a jot!
Ye problay could've been a Rangers hero, ye problay should've managed Scotland tae
But instid, yoo buhlt Fortress Tannadeechay, an gave the city thir second Discovery
Yir Mr Dundee United throo an throo, the blood in yir hert pumps tangerine
So heerz thanx fae Arabs past an prezzint — we knight yoo — arise Sir Jim McLean!

■ **Gary Robertson, poet, playwrite, author, Cundeez star, TV star.**

We want Jim, we want Jim!

FAN TRIBUTE: MIKE McDONALD, SHED BOY, DUNDEE.

ONE of my most cherished memories of Jim McLean is from after the UEFA Cup Final against Gothenburg in 1987.

A group of us stayed behind in The Shed after the game chanting Jim's name. "We want Jim, we want Jim, we want Jim!" we sang, over and over again.

After an hour of stewards and police unsuccessfully pleading with us to leave, Jim came back out, walking the whole length of the pitch to rapturous applause from his band of loyal Shed boys.

He thanked us for our magnificent support, but said it was time for us to go home.

A moment to cherish as we left with a smile on our faces and pride in our hearts.

May 20th, 1987. Jim comes out to talk to the fans in The Shed, long after the final whistle. It was the greatest night of football and sportsmanship that the city of Dundee has ever known.

JACKSON

Tannadice was a leap forward in time

PLAYER TRIBUTE: DAVE BOWMAN.

JIM McLEAN is often remembered as an old-school manager, a strict disciplinarian, and a man who was not in the habit of dishing out praise lightly.

For United old boy Dave Bowman, though, the words "ahead of his time" should always be added to the list of the great man's attributes.

Signed from Coventry City along with another United stalwart Jim McInally back in the summer of 1986 (a deal that cost just £140,000 for the pair) for "Bow" the move back to Tannadice and Scottish football – he'd started with Hearts – was not just a matter of a journey of a few hundred miles north, it was a leap forward in time.

"Right from the start at United, it was different to anything I'd known before and it was probably only later in my career I realised how far ahead of his time Jim was," says Dave.

"When I started doing coaching badges towards the end of my playing days we were being shown stuff that was being talked about as new, but we'd been doing it at United for years.

"In training and other areas Jim was always willing to try new things. I suppose we got so used to it we didn't realise it wasn't happening other places.

"In the eighties he was bringing in nutritionists and sports psychologists. I even remember one year he found out the winner of the marathon in the Olympics had worn a cotton shirt because he thought it was better for his performances than man-made fibres.

"The next thing we knew we were all wearing cotton tee-shirts under our tops. For a while we also had our own set of wee scales and were weighing our food and making sure we were eating the right stuff — again long before others were looking at that kind of thing.

"Did all the things he tried help? I'm sure some did and others didn't, but as a manager he was always willing to try anything to get even an extra 1% out of you that could mean the difference between winning and losing."

If McLean would experiment with anything he thought would help his beloved team, Dave stresses his old boss would prove just as quick to drop something if he felt it wasn't working.

"Back in '87 when we were drawn against Barcelona in the UEFA Cup, he had us working with psychologists for a few weeks. Everything was geared to getting us believing we could beat them and of course we did.

"The Saturday before the first leg, though, we went to Forfar in the Scottish Cup and almost lost. We only got a draw because of a very late penalty and after the game he told us that's the last we'd be seeing of the psychologist!"

It was later in that famous run to the UEFA Cup final

that Dave and his team-mates experienced a one-off from their manager.

"From your first day to your last at United, for Jim it was about how you could improve as a player and he wasn't one for handing out praise – he just kept on about where you could get better.

"There would be days when you knew you'd played well, but when you came off he would focus on a mistake you'd made or an area that had room for improvement.

"It was hard, but it was all about making you and the team better and I know I became a much better player because of him.

"He could also do things to help you, he just didn't let you know about it at the time. When I got into the Scotland squad, the game before I reported for duty I was dropped to the bench.

"I was thinking how am I going to get a game for Scotland when I can't even get a place in my club side? But I believe he knew I'd be starting for Scotland in the midweek and left me out to make sure I didn't get injured. That was the way he liked to do things.

"The one time he was different was when we reached the UEFA Cup final. We played Borussia Monchengladbach in the semis and after we beat them in the second leg over there he went round the dressing room and shook every one of us by the hand.

"That meant something. That handshake was a lot coming from him and it was a one-off, certainly for me. The one thing you knew about him was he treated everyone the same. If a kid made a mistake he'd get it in the ear and even the likes of Dave Narey – not that he made that many – would get exactly the same treatment if they got it wrong.

"It could be difficult when he was having a go at you, but when he was talking football everyone listened because you knew he knew exactly what he was talking about.

"And if you did listen you'd become better for it."

Family 1, Rangers 0 — a home win

FAN TRIBUTE: FRASER DURIE.

I MET Jim McLean in person in 1983 when I interviewed him for the Dundee Student newspaper, *Annasach*.

I was surprised but delighted when he agreed to be interviewed by a student instead of someone from a big newspaper, especially as this was right in the middle of the time when he was considering a potential move to become Rangers manager.

He firmly set the ground rules before the interview, though. He said that there was to be no discussion about Rangers or his eagerly-awaited decision on the potential move. He made it clear he wanted to talk only about United.

However, it wasn't long before he himself started talking about all his reasons for not making the move through to the west.

It was very clear to me that his passions were twofold, his family and Dundee United. There wasn't anything a bigger club could offer to him that he hadn't got already.

I left the interview, which lasted well over an hour and included meeting the chairman and seeing the league trophy, struggling to match the public persona with this warm and generous man I had just met.

I had sat entranced by his obvious love of the game and of his club and his incredible knowledge of football.

It struck me at the time there was so much more to the man than the public persona that was often presented in the press.

I'm sure he was difficult and grumpy at times, he was doing a very intense job after all. But there was also much more than that beneath the surface.

The article appeared in *Annasach* and I was really proud of it. But a friend at the time told me that it didn't fit with the usual newspaper profile of Jim McLean, so it was unlikely to be printed anywhere other than the student paper!

■ This photo is dated May 4th, 1971, and was taken at Tay Bridge Railway Station. Jim, Dundee FC first-team coach at the time, says goodbye to his family as he is off to Portugal to take part in a tournament involving Sporting Lisbon, Vitoria de Setubal and Norwich City.

Player 'favour' Jim did for Dundee FC

TRIBUTE: PETER MARR.

THAT for Jim McLean Dundee United came first there can be no question. From the moment he walked into Tannadice as manager towards the end of 1971, the Tangerines were his number one priority and would remain so for the next three decades.

He quickly became known for his determination to make United as good as they possibly could be and in doing so at times an impression grew that nothing else, in football terms at least, mattered to him.

The fact he worked for a time as part-time assistant to the great Jock Stein with the Scotland set up gives a strong indication that was not, in fact, the case.

As is recorded elsewhere in this book, down the years players and coaches who'd moved on from United also benefited from his willingness to provide help and advice.

Even those who did not work closely with him at Tannadice received his valuable help.

Some staunch United fans may be surprised to learn those among that select and fortunate band included some of those who found themselves operating just over the road at Dens Park, home of city rivals Dundee FC.

Former Dundee owner Peter Marr is more than happy to pay tribute to the great man's work.

Shortly after, along with his brother Jimmy, becoming Dark Blues owner, Peter sat down with McLean to pick his brains and left Tannadice not just with some valuable information but also with advice on a player who would go on to serve the Dark Blues well.

"When Jimmy and I took over, two men we contacted to see if they had any advice that might help us were Jim McLean at United and Geoff Brown at St Johnstone," recalls Peter.

"It was one of those things where if they had said they couldn't help us we would have understood, but it was typical of both that they took the time to meet us and give a very good idea about what we could expect as owners.

"When we met Jim at Tannadice he didn't just give us advice, he actually let us now about a player he thought could be a very good signing for Dundee.

"It was Steven Boyack who was playing in Rangers reserves at the time and United had been looking at him. But United already had a few players who operated in his area of the park and Jim and his scouts decided that Steven was perhaps not any better than he already had in his squad.

"He could have said nothing about it because he'd be helping his city rivals, but Jim saw the chance to help us, and Steven Boyack as well, and told us he would do a good job for us. Boyack turned out to be a

Peter Marr – competitive, but civil.

great player for us and I've never forgotten what Jim did for us."

By the time Peter was at Dens, Jim's time as United manager was over and he was club chairman. Once Dundee were back in the Premier League and meetings during Dundee derbies became regular features on Dundee's football calendar again, the rivalry between the two boardrooms may have been highly competitive, but it remained civil.

"We were always made very welcome at Tannadice and Jim would always take time to have a chat and ask how things were going. There were even times when I would go to Tannadice for games we weren't involved in and he always made a point of inviting me to the boardroom.

"Jim McLean is a football person and although he put Dundee United first, as he was right to do, if he could help others he would. Like Geoff Brown he had huge experience of the game and what it took to run a club. These guys knew how hard it could be and always showed an understanding of that when they were dealing with us. It's why they are two men I have huge respect for to this day."

And while he remains a Dundee man, Peter has no qualms about rating Jim McLean as one of Scottish football's greats.

"He did an amazing job as manager and, for me, as chairman. When I was a boy Dundee United were hardly mentioned as a force in the game, but Jim came in, grabbed United by the seat of their pants and made them into a major force.

"He won the League and the League Cup, came close in the Scottish Cup a few times and was not far away from lifting two European trophies and in the process made a lot of money for United by producing and selling very good players when he had to.

"Even though I'm a Dundee FC man I think it would have been fitting if he'd lifted the Scottish Cup as manager to complete the set of domestic trophies."

Star-struck at Tannadice Park

FAN TRIBUTE: ANDREW MEAKIN.

I REMEMBER persuading my father to drive me from Crieff for a derby at Dens in December or January in the mid-1980s.

The game was called off very late because of a frozen pitch so I took the opportunity to nip into the ticket office at Tannadice to buy tickets for an upcoming Celtic game.

There was a small queue, probably just five or six of us. While we waited, Jim appeared behind the glass to speak to one of the staff, then disappeared again.

Next thing we knew he had emerged and took a few minutes to walk along the line to have a word with each of us, complaining about the late call off, hoping we hadn't travelled far and suchlike.

He didn't have to do that, but the fact that he did said a lot about the man. I left, clutching my tickets, star-struck!

FAN TRIBUTE: CHARLES STIRTON.

IF it wasn't for Jim McLean, where would United be now? The man's a legend.

FAN TRIBUTE: Mrs MARGARET STEVENSON.

I SAW your request for people to say their piece about Mr Jim McLean and I have always wanted to give my point of view.

I'm not a football supporter at all, though my son-in-law would go to all Dundee United's games. But I have read, and people have said to me, that Mr McLean was a coarse and angry sort of man. But this is not at all true.

I worked for the Ninewells Blood Transfusion Service and Mr McLean came to donate a pint of blood at a mobile session we had at Radio Tay's premises, in 1983. He was extremely polite, and interested in what the transfusion service did. He didn't flinch a bit when I put the needle in to take the blood.

He was a most pleasant man and smiled all the time, even though I was twittering like a budgie at him. I still have the article about that day, which was printed in the Evening Telegraph.

■ Right: Margaret checking Jim's blood pressure in the 1983 photo that was published in the Tele.

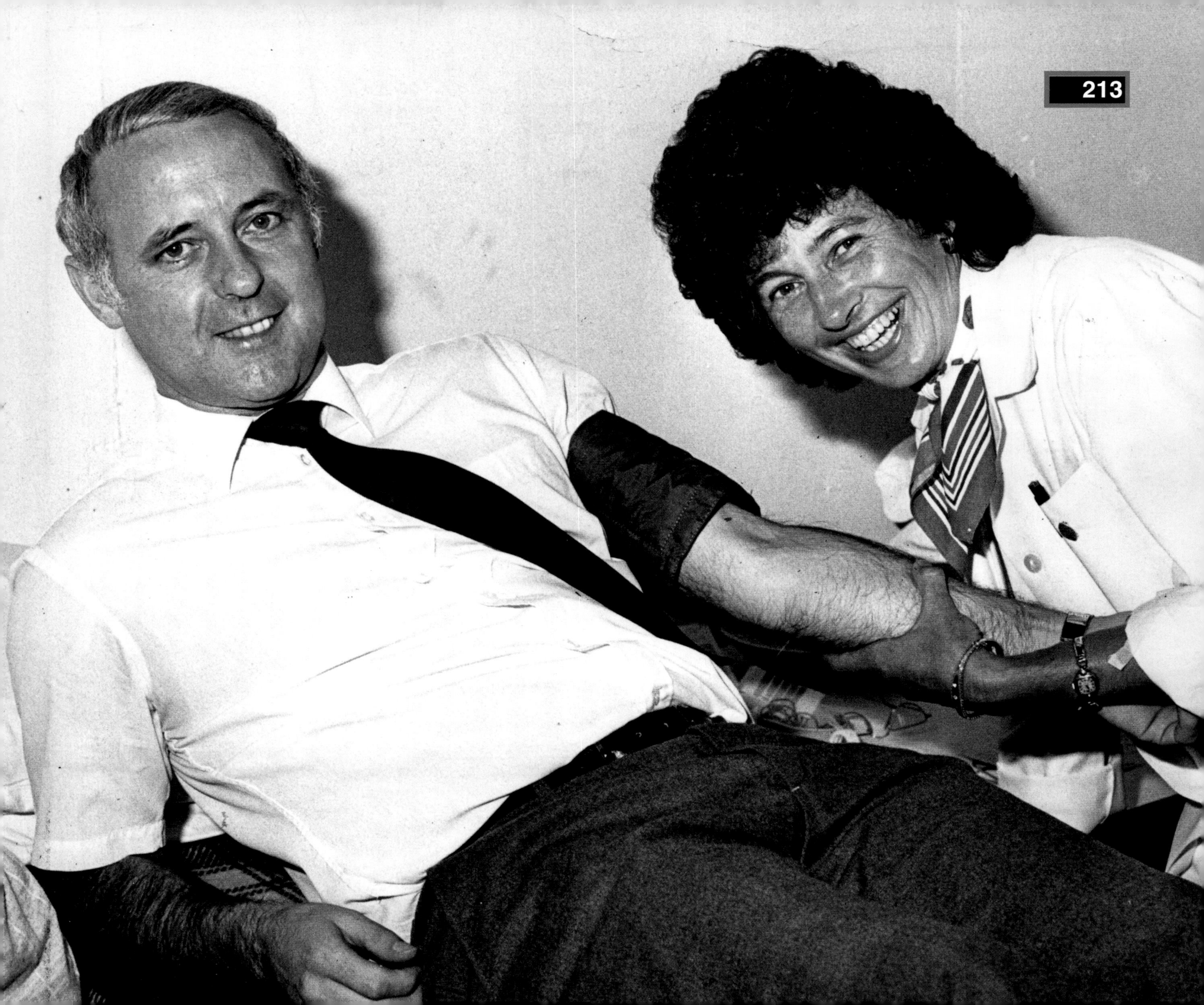
213

A night out in 1979. The fashion police were called just after this photo was taken, and several arrests were made.

■ Dens Park, April 20th, 1993. Dundee FC vice-chairman Malcolm Reid presented a decanter and glasses to mark the last time a Jim McLean-managed side would play a derby. United won 4-0.

Jim McLean was how we saw manhood

TRIBUTE: NEIL FORSYTH, AUTHOR OF THE BOB SERVANT BOOKS.

WE live in a time riven with superficiality and fleetingness. Newspapers, books, prolonged moments of mental silence, all swamped by the urgent irrelevance of social media.

Football has changed accordingly.

Managers come and go so rapidly you can forget they were ever there. These days, a slow-burn type of success would be extinguished long before it sparked into life.

Jim McLean represents a different time.

A time of permanence. A time when, for an entire childhood and teenage years, your football club could have one manager.

Time passed slowly under McLean. Seasons came and went as he stood glowering at the side of the pitch, feathering the nest of his legend.

For my generation, his impact was formative. He was how we saw football. He was how we saw manhood. And the game doesn't make men like that anymore. There isn't the time.

He was a coiled spring of hunger and anger and determination, who rose in the morning wounded and seeking revenge.

And his revenge was to take a provincial football club and drag them to domestic glory and on to impossible foreign adventures.

His revenge was to give an awed set of supporters a set of experiences that would mark heavily upon their lives.

He taught us to fight against the natural order.

He taught us that the world, that vast, murky, unknown pre-Internet world, was not to be feared but to be invaded and conquered.

He taught us that our club mattered. That our city mattered. That we mattered.

He raged and fought and scrapped and roused a band of men into feats that should have been far beyond them.

And I hope it didn't cost him too much.

I hope that Jim McLean remembers who he is. I hope that he remembers what he did. And I hope that he knows that he is a hero.

Like all men, he is many things. But Jim McLean is truly a hero.

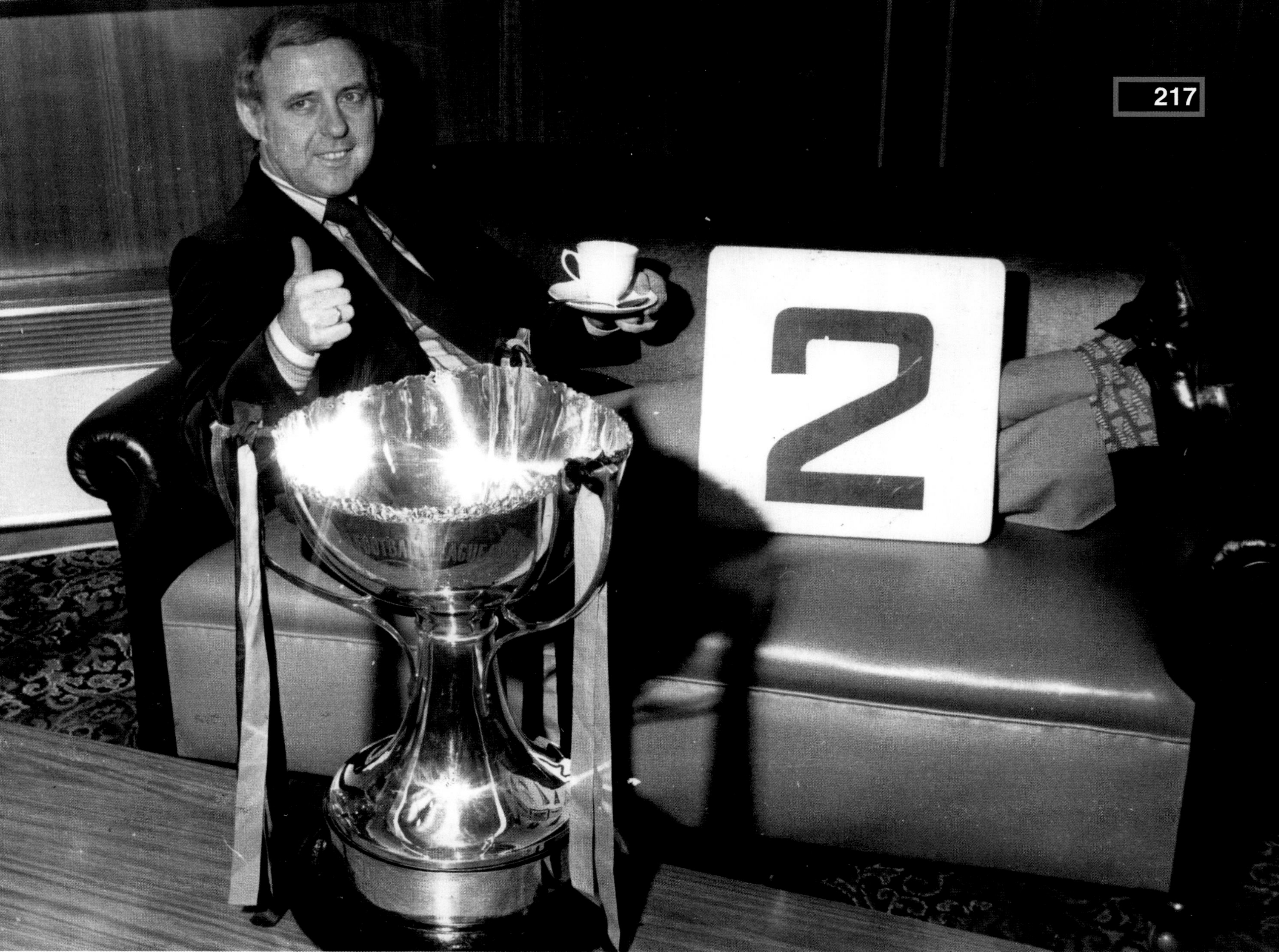

This was Jim's revenge. He made Dundee United into serial winners This was his second League Cup, celebrated with a cup of tea. (Photo courtesy of Fotopress.)

Looking out for his boys

FOOTBALL is a fleeting career. Even the greats, the long-serving players with 800+ games under their belt, will usually finish playing at some point in their thirties.

What do they do after that?

Nowadays, there is more money in the game. But in the 1970s and '80s players often had to quickly find another job if they weren't carrying on as coaches, managers or pundits.

Jim arranged evening classes for his players, educating them and preparing them for the days after The Shed had stopped chanting their names.

November 1981. United players (and a couple of Dundee players invited along too) during a business studies course at Bell Street College of Technology. Their tutor was Mr Aubrey Hughes (standing).

Ralph Milne

Jim and Fergie, mutual respect

TRIBUTE: RADIO PERSONALITY RICHARD GORDON.

AS a young fan growing up in Aberdeen, I quickly developed a voracious appetite for the game and became aware of the other sides around the country.

At the time, Dundee were the biggest team on Tayside. They weren't at the same level they had been in the early 1960s, but a decade on still had some good players, and beat Jock Stein's Celtic to win the League Cup in 1973. Back then, United barely registered.

Jim McLean had replaced Jerry Kerr as manager at Tannadice a couple of years previously, but any work going on behind the scenes had yet to reap dividends, and it wasn't until they reached the Scottish Cup Final in '74 that I really became aware that something might just be stirring down the road from Dens.

It was to take a few more years and a near relegation – ironically, Dundee went down when reconstruction brought the advent of the new-look Premier Division – but the United revolution was gathering pace, and by then everyone with an interest in Scottish football knew who McLean was.

As he pieced together what would be the club's greatest-ever team, Jim very much did it his way and dictated everything that happened. He ruled by fear, but also respect, and stories of how he ran the club are legendary.

As a Dons fan, I was intrigued by his rivalry with Alex Ferguson, but it wasn't until many years later, having had the opportunity to interview both men and speak to those who were close to them back then, that I began to comprehend the lengths each would go to in an attempt to outdo the other. Their will to win was imbued deep in their souls, they were perfectionists, and they expected that approach from their players and staff.

Over the eight years they went head to head as Aberdeen and United managers, each enjoyed spells of dominance. United often had better results at Pittodrie, the Dons down at Tannadice, and every 90 minutes was a tactical battle between two of the sharpest football minds this country has ever produced.

The big breakthrough for Jim came in the 1979-80 League Cup, ironically enough against his big rival. I was at both games that winter of '79. Aberdeen should have won the initial encounter at Hampden but United blew them away in the replay at Dens Park, and McLean finally had a tangible reward for almost a decade of unrelenting hard toil building up the club.

It was, of course, a first major honour for Dundee United, but while they would repeat the win 12 months later and go on to clinch the league title in 1983, I have always felt three trophies was scant reward for Jim and that remarkable team.

He had some excellent players, but he also had a number of less talented individuals who he somehow drove to greater heights than they might have achieved elsewhere, or under any other manager.

That probably says more about Jim's abilities than anything, and some of the results and performances his United side put in throughout the 1980s were absolutely astonishing. They should have been in the 1984 European Cup Final; they came agonisingly close to winning the 1987 UEFA Cup. When younger United fans ponder that, they must shake their heads in bewilderment. But to those of us who were around back then, who saw that team in action, what they did came as no surprise – they were one helluva side.

By the mid to late eighties I had somehow got a job at Northsound Radio. This was long before the days of structured weekly media conferences in front of sponsors' advertising boards; back then, when I wanted a preview interview ahead of one of United's big games, I simply had to call the Tannadice switchboard and ask to be put through to the great man.

I was a cub reporter, and I have to admit to feeling a little anxious as I waited to hear his familiar gruff tones at the end of the line. However, he never refused to talk, and as soon as he did start answering my questions his love of the game shone through. I wouldn't go as far as to say that I ever felt totally comfortable making those calls, but I always looked forward to hearing what he had to say.

Throughout this book you will read testimonials from those who knew him far better than I ever did, but I will guarantee that one theme will run through all of them.

His players lived in fear of disappointing him, but to this day each and every one of them retain a love and respect for the man, and acknowledge the part he played in making them the players and men they grew to be.

Jim McLean and Alex Ferguson. Friends and rivals, and a great deal of mutual respect.

Sir Alex Ferguson is, for me, the greatest ever Scottish football manager. His old friend and rival, Jim McLean, is not far behind.

Jim — nursing home fire hero

IN May 2005, Jim played a part in rescuing people from a burning nursing home, next to the bowling green where he was taking part in a game.

Jim really enjoyed bowling and was a member at Broughty Bowling Club, off Claypotts Road. Indeed, along with playing partner Neil Alexander, a former policeman, he made it to the final of the club's two-ball pairs and chose to write about this in a column he used to do for a west coast newspaper. Like every sporting encounter he ever had, Jim took his "bools" very seriously, but claimed he was "being carried" by Neil.

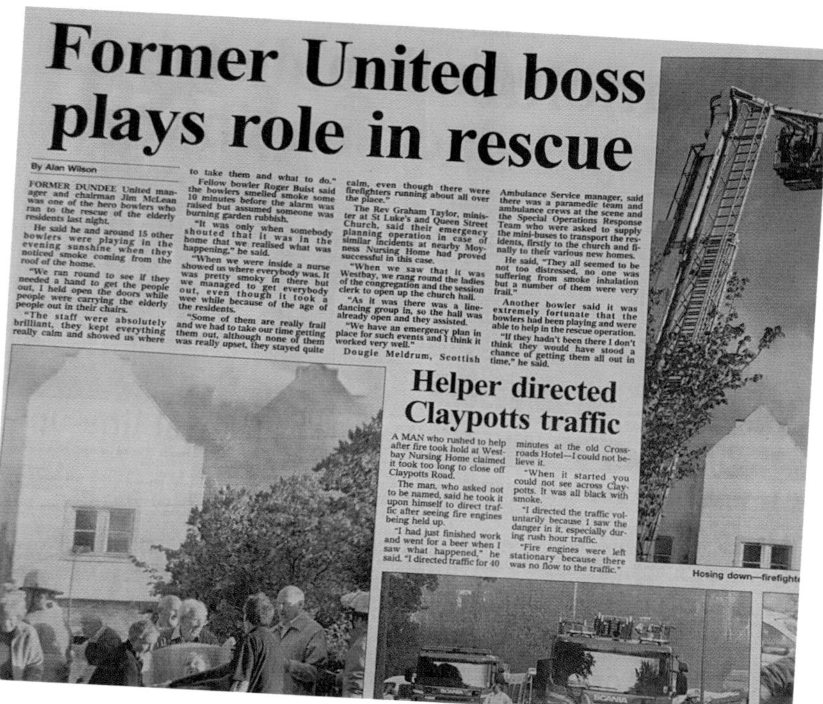

Former United boss plays role in rescue

By Alan Wilson

FORMER DUNDEE United manager and chairman Jim McLean was one of the hero bowlers who ran to the rescue of the elderly residents last night.

He said he and around 15 other bowlers were playing in the evening sunshine when they noticed smoke coming from the roof of the home.

"We ran round to see if they needed a hand to get the people out. I held open the doors while people were carrying the elderly people out in their chairs.

"The staff were absolutely brilliant, they kept everything really calm and showed us where to take them and what to do."

Fellow bowler Roger Buist said the bowlers smelled smoke some 10 minutes before the alarm was raised but assumed someone was burning garden rubbish.

"It was only when somebody shouted that it was in the home that we realised what was happening," he said.

"When we were inside a nurse showed us where everybody was. It was pretty smoky in there but we managed to get everybody out, even though it took a wee while because of the age of the residents.

"Some of them are really frail and we had to take our time getting them out, although none of them was really upset, they stayed quite calm, even though there were firefighters running about all over the place."

The Rev Graham Taylor, minister at St Luke's and Queen Street Church, said their emergency planning operation in case of similar incidents at nearby Moyness Nursing Home had proved successful in this case.

"When we saw that it was Westbay, we rang round the ladies of the congregation and the session clerk to open up the church hall.

"As it was there was a line-dancing group in, so the hall was already open and they assisted.

"We have an emergency plan in place for such events and I think it worked very well."

Dougie Meldrum, Scottish Ambulance Service manager, said there was a paramedic team and ambulance crews at the scene and the Special Operations Response Team who were asked to supply the mini-buses to transport the residents, firstly to the church and finally to their various new homes.

He said, "They all seemed to be not too distressed, no one was suffering from smoke inhalation but a number of them were very frail."

Another bowler said it was extremely fortunate that the bowlers had been playing and were able to help in the rescue operation.

"If they hadn't been there I don't think they would have stood a chance of getting them all out in time," he said.

Helper directed Claypotts traffic

A MAN who rushed to help after fire took hold at Westbay Nursing Home claimed it took too long to close off Claypotts Road.

The man, who asked not to be named, said he took it upon himself to direct traffic after seeing fire engines being held up.

"I had just finished work and went for a beer when I saw what happened," he said. "I directed traffic for 40 minutes at the old Crossroads Hotel—I could not believe it.

"When it started you could not see across Claypotts. It was all black with smoke.

"I directed the traffic voluntarily because I saw the danger in it, especially during rush hour traffic.

"Fire engines were left stationary because there was no flow to the traffic."

Hosing down—firefight

■ **The Courier's inside-page report of the nursing home fire.**

But on the occasion of the fire, the early-evening game was rapidly abandoned as the smoke poured out next door, and Jim's pairs match players rushed to help evacuate the elderly people.

This was a big fire, front-page news at the time. The aerial views of the burned-out home, with its collapsed roof, were striking. At one point, there were 60-foot flames shooting into the night sky. One resident was taken to hospital, complaining of chest pains.

So it isn't overly-dramatic to say that the swift action of Jim and his fellow bowlers, several minutes before the Fire Brigade arrived, was instrumental in saving lives. A total of 33 frail old folk, some of whom used wheelchairs to get about, in all their separate rooms in a large, smoke-filled building, is a recipe for disaster.

Jim, in typical modest fashion, played down his role, saying he "just held open doors" and helped the residents gather a safe distance from the smoke. He preferred to heap praise on the home's staff, and paid further tribute to the calm way the residents coped with the situation.

But by any measure, Jim is a rescue hero not just a football hero.

■ The bowling club team fire heroes, from left: Jim McLean, Jim Doig, Bill McKail and Jim Reid.

Jim McLean — tennis ace

TRIBUTE: DAVID GORDON.

EVERY sport that is played with a ball requires two basic skills: a good sense of timing, and good hand-eye (or foot-eye in the case of football) coordination.

You often find that people who are good at football are also good at other ball sports, such as golf, or find dancing easy to pick up. They are used to their body just "knowing" what to do when playing sport.

It won't surprise you to learn, then, that Jim was very good at golf, and enjoyed the game, but he excelled at tennis.

While he was still a coach at Dens, Jim, with Jocky Scott and Jim Steele, went along to Forthill Tennis Club in the close season to play a few balls over the net and keep their fitness up before pre-season training started.

Many footballers used to keep themselves in shape over the long summers, as they knew they'd go back to managers and coaches who would delight in making them run until they threw up.

Dave Gordon, who ran the tennis teams at Forthill back then, saw these lads playing and reckoned that while Jocky and Jim Steele weren't bad at all, Jim McLean stood out as "a natural".

Dave approached the three, had a chat, and persuaded them to play for Forthill, when training and football matches left them available for the games, on Tuesdays and Thursdays, in the local tennis league.

So they did.

Jim was so good that he made it to the first team. "He hated to lose," David said. "He'd do his very best in every game, which is what you want when there are league standings at stake.

"We became quite friendly. For about 20 years I'd go up to Tannadice and take part in some of the fitness training. The all-round conditioning the footballers got was very good, very impressive.

"I went to Sweden with the team for the UEFA Cup Final. When we got to the training facility some of the lads thought it would be a good idea to throw me in the swimming pool. Fully clothed.

"I was like a drowned rat. That Dave Bowman, he was the ring-leader!

"I didn't have any other clothes with me, so the reception staff dried my tracksuit and loaned me a dressing gown while they were doing it.

"Jim saw me wearing this gown, and I think he must have guessed what happened. He found it extremely funny anyway!"

■ **Jim taking part in a tournament semi-final in 1973. (Pic courtesy of Dave Martin, Fotopress.)**

Jim was 'that manager' for United

TRIBUTE: ARCHIE MACPHERSON, SCOTLAND'S FAVOURITE TV COMMENTATOR

"MILNE…wriggles clear…might just get the chip… and he does! He's scored. Oh what a great goal." Archie Macpherson owns a place in Dundee United folklore. His BBC Sportscene commentary is the soundtrack to THAT goal on THAT day in May 1983.

And Archie, a man always worth listening to when he talks about football, has firm opinions, and a high regard, for the knowledge Jim McLean had.

In Archie's words:

JIM McLEAN is without doubt the most interesting man I've ever discussed football with.

He could be abrupt at times, but when he got talking you found he had a uniquely analytical brain when it comes to players and the game.

His delivery was usually in a monotone manner. He wasn't in any way an animated talker. But when you listened to the words he was saying, his thoughts were amazingly perceptive. He would dissect players and teams. Few managers I have ever known could do that to the same degree. Perhaps Jock Stein was as good at examining and explaining players' strengths and weaknesses. But the way Jim did it was very impressive. Anyone hearing him talk, and thinking about what he was saying, wouldn't forget it.

I had some hugely interesting discussions with him, especially on the European trips that became such a feature for Dundee United all through the 1980s.

Of course, along with Alex Ferguson when Fergie was at Aberdeen, Jim harboured a strong feeling that the west coast media didn't give any other teams as much credit as they deserved. They just wanted to talk and write about the Old Firm all the time, no matter how they were playing, no matter how other teams were playing. Both men resented that.

And they had a point, Jim especially. United were a small, parochial club that no one in the west wanted to have in the elite positions in Scottish football. People thought of them as a small club, getting in the way of the Old Firm. But Jim changed all that. He forced United's way into the heart of the Scottish game. He took them right to the top.

I have the greatest respect for men like Stein, and Willie Waddell, Rangers' European trophy-winning manager. Jim's work was of a different type, but just as impressive.

Lifting Dundee United up from what they were to what they became is one of the great achievements in Scottish football.

Jock Stein chose him to be assistant Scotland manager, and that was a huge thing and a great accolade. That speaks volumes for him.

Who would have thought that Dundee United would have made it to the semi-final of the most prestigious club competition in world football? It was an astonishing transformation from where he started. No one would have given United a chance of doing that. It is perhaps only now, looking back, that it is dawning on some people just how astonishing this was.

That game in Rome, though, the second leg of the European Cup semi-final, was a game I will never forget.

I was doing the commentary and it was a truly frightening experience. As bad as I have ever seen at any football match in my life. There were lethal things been thrown from all angles, not just paper cups or small items. It was mayhem. People crowding round very aggressively. It was an ugly situation after the final whistle, a dangerous situation. Not just noisy as other grounds were. You expect noise and verbal aggression in any football ground. This was different.

There was an intent to do damage or draw blood that I have never seen in any ground in Europe. And the policing was terrible. Non-existent. It should never have been allowed to happen like that.

Another thing Jim really didn't like was the 10-team Premier League, from 1975 onwards. He thought it set the game in Scotland back by years.

He'd say Celtic and Rangers had no chance of being relegated, but every one of the other eight clubs couldn't be sure. It turned into a league of two trying to win it,

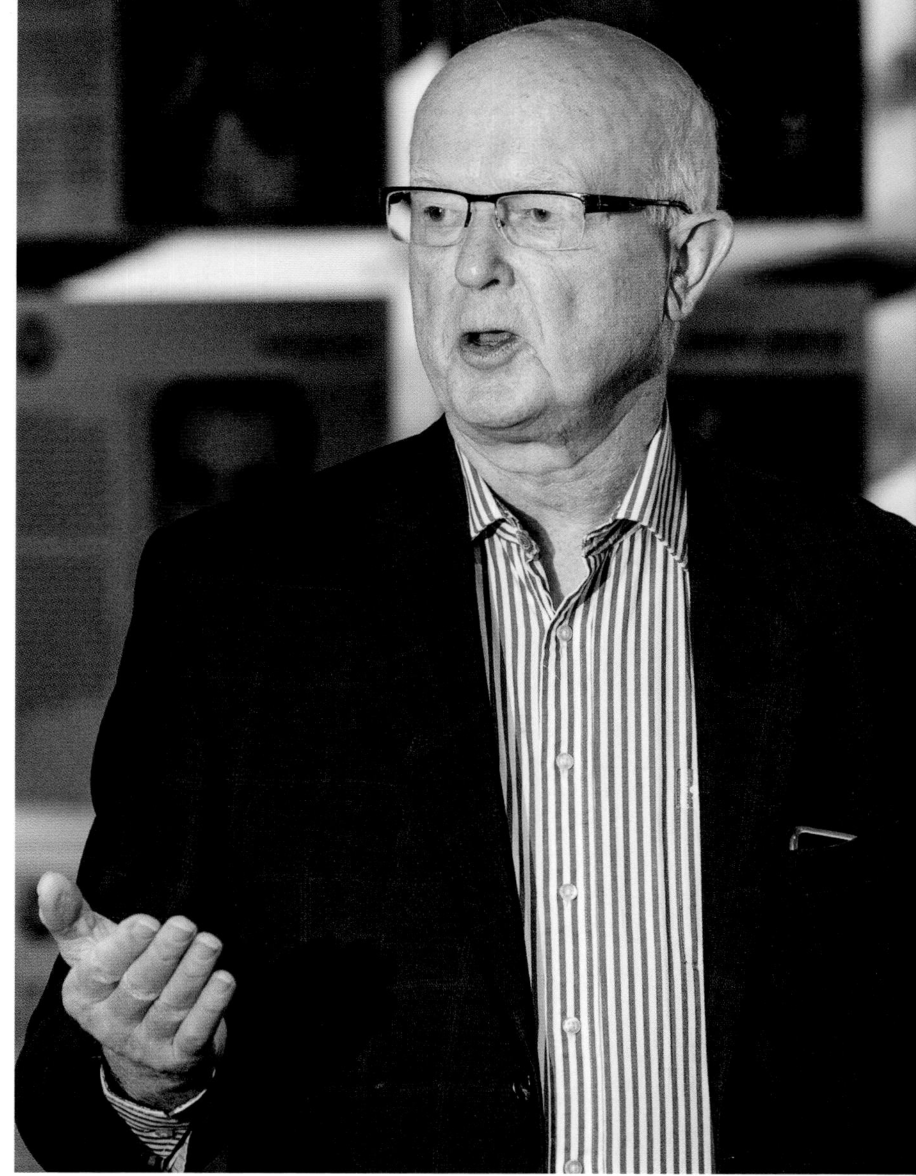

and a league of eight trying not to be relegated. He gave the example of Graeme Payne. A great player. Much like Gordon Strachan, though not with Strachan's snap and bite. But a superb football player in his own right that we never saw the best of in the Scottish game.

Payne was kicked out of football. There was no room

left in the defensive, aggressive, Premier League for an artist like that. In another league, perhaps in a different era, he would have been an international superstar.

But Jim told me that he couldn't get Payne on the ball in United's midfield.

In fact Jim, during one of his more bitter moments, once said to me he was going to get United playing a long-ball game, missing out the midfield altogether, because that was the only way to succeed in the dour, cynical game that Scottish football had become.

He didn't mean it of course, he was expressing his disgust at the lack of football that was being played at our stadiums. The game was, he believed, entertainment. Or should be.

Jim knew what he was talking about. He was always worth listening to because he saw things so clearly. He could see right through a game of football as if he had X-ray vision.

You see, some people talk a good game. They will tell you this and that about how football should be played, mostly after a game has finished. And give their opinion of what a player had done or should have done. But Jim could send a team out knowing in advance what would happen. That's a very different thing.

You'll hear pundits on TV who make it sound easy, but it certainly isn't easy. Jim had that extra dimension that lifted him above the ordinary run of managers. He was the opposite of just a talker, he was a creator.

Lawrie McMenemy, the great FA Cup-winning Southampton manager, once pointed out a truism about football to me, and he mentioned Jim McLean when he was saying this.

He said that sometimes a "that manager" era will raise a club up. It certainly doesn't happen to every club, but there are several examples.

It happens when a club has a time when it has one manager, "that" manager, that one man who just makes it happen at that club. All the stars align. Right man, right club, right type of players, right time.

Men like Brian Clough at Nottingham Forest winning the league and two European Cups, or Dave Bowen taking Northampton Town from the English Fourth Division to the First in five seasons. And you'd have to include Dave Bassett, with his particularly robust brand of football that suited Wimbledon and the players he had, and that took them from the Fourth to the First Division in England.

That's what Dundee United had, Lawrie said, in Jim McLean. It is a very rare thing.

And, in truth, the club have been trying to find a new Jim McLean ever since. They have had a succession of managers trying to recapture that blend.

But then all clubs would have liked to have had a Jim McLean in their history.

■ **Graeme Payne in full flow (although flagged offside, on this occasion you'll notice). He might have been an international superstar, but for Scotland's brutal Premier League. The pic carries instructional marks, having had a long working life in a newspaper archive.**

LOTTERY
TSB

If he'd gone south

ANALYSIS: STEVE FINAN.

BRIAN CLOUGH brought Nottingham Forest to Tannadice for Jim's testimonial game in August 1984. It was hardly a full-paced game, but United won 2-0. Terry Venables brought Barcelona to Tannadice in 1987. United won 1-0.

So how might Jim have done against these sort of managers if he had moved south? He had the opportunity to do so, having been offered the jobs of managing Newcastle United and Chelsea.

Perhaps, like Fergie, he would have taken a few years to bed in at an English club. But the core traits of any team he ever put on the park – that they be fitter than the opposition, that they keep the ball as much, maintained a solid defensive shape at all times, and had genuine pace up front to attack – would surely have brought success. Indeed, the one time he faced an English club in anger, in 1984, his high-pressing tactics gave Ron Atkinson's Manchester United a real fright at Old Trafford.

The 2-2 draw might have shocked English TV commentators, it didn't surprise anyone in Scotland.

We'll never know what he might have done, of course (thank goodness!) But it's an intriguing question. Say he'd gone to a club with the potential of Newcastle United when they asked him.

It is a city obsessed with football, but burdened with a continually under-achieving team. They'd have loved Jim's incredible commitment to the job, talent-spotting skills, tactical genius, and fitter-than-the-rest players.

Fergie's so-called mind-games certainly wouldn't have worked on Jim the way they (legend has it) worked on Kevin Keegan.

The only question, I reckon, is just how many cups and titles Newcastle would have won.

Jim's attention to video analysis

FAN TRIBUTE: CHRIS ROY.

I WORKED with Jim on a voluntary basis for many years providing video of games.

He was way ahead of his time in the way he used this footage, often asking me to film very specific things like the back four or full-back overlaps. Even on one occasion following one player for 45 minutes to assess his work-rate off the ball.

Jim's attention to detail was incredible. For a good few years the video was delivered to him straight after games, sometimes I'd catch him before he left Tannadice, if not I delivered it to his house.

The time commitment he gave the club and the high standards he expected from everyone, however you were involved, was a huge part of the success our club achieved under his leadership.

Jim simply was the best in his field.

I remember a night at Meadowbank when an upcoming touchline ban meant the testing of new radios.

I went through with Jim and Luggy in Luggy's car to a reserve game.

The first half was 0-0 and Jim was far from happy. "Come wi' me," he said "And I'll show you how we get this lot working."

I witnessed Jim in full flow in the Portacabin dressing rooms. Finally threatening to fine them all their week's wages if they didn't get their fingers out.

On his way past a shell-shocked me, he winked. Funnily enough United ran out comfortable winners.

He really was something else and, as I knew him, he also had a very funny, dry sense of humour.

FAN TRIBUTE: BRUCE LINDSAY.

ONE memory of Jim that stands out for me was back in 1979-80.

It was a home game and we were standing on The High Terrace, which is now the George Fox Stand.

Jim had been banned from the touchline so he was sitting in the stand behind the dugouts.

We could see him standing up and shouting and gesticulating at the bench, but they obviously couldn't hear him.

Next thing there was a wee lull in the crowd noise and even from the other side of the ground we could clearly hear Jim shout, "Wattie, get f***** Bannon aff".

■ Jim's preparation and attention to detail was second to none. This is an early-morning pic taken at Scone Aerodrome, in October 1983, showing the United and Aberdeen scouting parties off to run the rule over their next European opponents. United had drawn Standard Liege, of Belgium, in the European Cup. The Dons were playing SK Beveren, also of Belgium, in their defence of the Cup Winners' Cup. From left: Gordon Wallace, Walter Smith, Jim McLean, Alex Ferguson and Archie Knox. Both sides made it through to the next round. (Pic courtesy of Dave Martin, Fotopress.)

Jim looking tickled pink at winning the League Cup in 1979.

There can surely be nothing better than winning a cup at your local rivals' ground . . . unless, of course, you could win the League Championship at their ground!

DUFC
LEAGUE CUP
FINAL 1979/80
adidas

Jim's tactics, on the buses

FAN TRIBUTE: CRAIG MITCHELL.

I'M just about to turn 60 and Dundee United have contributed a lot to my life, with Jim McLean a central figure. One story I always tell goes back to September 1982 when my friend Brian Ross and I travelled with the team to the epic Eindhoven away game, and set off by coach from Tannadice.

We were in row 2. In front of us were Jim and Walter Smith. It was a dreich day so all the coach windows misted up.

Travelling down the M90, the next thing we see is Jim using the steamed-up window as if it was a tactics board, working out formations and moves.

He never relaxed, he was the lifeblood of United. The bus tactics obviously worked because United beat the Dutch giants 2-0. What a team they were.

FAN TRIBUTE: JOHNNY M, EX-LOCHEE.

THE thing I love about Jim McLean is that he gave United all the bragging rights in the city of Dundee.

When I was at school, Dundee were the "big team" and won the league. But all that has all turned around completely. As United's victories and trophies piled up, Dundee's place in the game in Scotland has gone down by miles. So now we have all the trump cards in every argument between football fans because we can say, "We won the league at Dens".

There is nothing that they can say that beats that.

We became champions of Scotland on their midden. We went there and celebrated all around their ground, that was full of Arabs that day. I was there, we filled the Provie. We took it over.

I never bothered arguing with Celtic and Rangers fans in my work, they only care about each other's teams. They can go away and join the English Premier League for all I care. No loss.

And Aberdeen or St Johnstone aren't really our derby, Dundee FC is our derby. That's what football is all about. It's about talking and arguing with your mates and workmates. That's what you spend all your time doing. We've got all the funny songs to sing at derbies, and we're always giving them a hammering.

All the kids growing up in the 1980s and 1990s became United supporters. And all their kids are now United supporters. It's because Jim McLean got United to all those cup finals and made all the European runs. We became the town's big club. Still are, always will be.

Thank you very much for all of that Sir Jim.

■ **We won the league at Dens, fly the flag, fly the flag.**

DEI DONUM

■ August 1st, 1993. The beginning of a new era. This is the United squad Jim passed on to his successor.

■ Back, from left: Mark Perry, John Clark, James Morrison, Guido van der Kamp, Brian Welsh, Alan Main, Stuart Garden, Christian Dailly, David Hannah.

■ Third row: Jim McInally, Chris Myers, Paddy Connolly, Billy McKinlay, Alec Cleland, Grant Johnson, Scott Crabbe.

■ Second row: Graham Liveston (head of youth development), Gregor Benvie, Eddie Conville, Kevin Biggart, Robbie Winters, Tom McMillan, Robert Stevenson, Roy McBain, John Lindsay, Steven Agnew, Gerry Borland, Ryan Hegarty, Andrew Cargill, Neill Devlin, John Sharp (physio),
■ Front: Paul Sturrock (coach), Michael O'Neill, John O'Neil, Dave Bowman, Andy McLaren, Ivan Golac (manager), Maurice Malpas, Freddie van der Hoorn, Gary Bollan, Dave Narey, Paul Hegarty (coach).

Smile was more than just a play

WE ardent Arabs, we're football people. And the supporter's world is a hard place, often an angry, shouting, gesticulating, snarling place.

Football is about tribalism, victory chants and the dirges of defeat. It's about a will to win, going "in where it hurts", and baying for the blood of referees.

What the hell has our football world got to do with a play in a theatre? How could the events of our world be represented by pose-about actors on a cosy stage? What would effete mummers know about Jim McLean's white-hot desire for a Dundee United away win at Ibrox?

An awful lot, it turns out.

The reaction to Phil Differ's play, *Smile*, in which he explored the complex character of Jim McLean, was really quite remarkable.

The Dundee public embraced it in a way that few, if any, stage productions in the city had ever managed before. *Smile* sold almost every one of The Rep's 450 seats for every performance of the 2020 run.

The really unusual thing, though, was that footsoldier Arabs "felt" it. It's one thing to impress regular theatre-goers, it is quite another to pull in non-theatre-going people and put a tear in their eye and fire in their belly.

Smile gave another layer of history to the football club, the legend of "the world famous" was added to.

The play also deepened the mystique of Dundee United and Jim McLean. Better still, *Smile* strengthened the already powerful place Dundee United has in the psyche of the city. But *Smile* did more than that. It also strengthened the city itself.

Ach, it was just a play, aye? Players that strut and fret their hour upon the stage and then are heard no more.

No.

Too often Dundee has put itself down. Perhaps we grew used to other people doing that. Perhaps we are guilty of doing it ourselves. The importance of this play in changing the pattern cannot be underestimated. *Smile* helped lead us to a corner.

Dundee had long been dragging itself out of its post-industrial slumber when this play debuted, of course, and doing it well. The town is different now, and *Smile* was another step, another rung.

But it was a play, just a play, only a play.

Yes. Although, when you think about it, we'd never really had anything like this before. What other book, play or film had reached in to grab a part of the fabric of oor toon and displayed it in such an inspiring light?

Name another Dundee United play that has done that? Name any play that has done that?

We Dundonians rarely think about exactly why we should have confidence in the city. And passion. And a feeling of self-worth. And reasons to straighten our backs, lift our chins and say "Aye, we're fae Dundee".

That's what the arts can do. That's what a play, a sculpture, a story can do.

These things hold up a mirror to a city.

Perhaps surprisingly, the reflection shows much to be proud of, much to celebrate, many achievements to recall, and the images of great sons and daughters who etched their mark on the place. It helps us see the best of ourselves, and ourselves as we'd like others to see us.

This image showed us Jim McLean, a mercurial, proud man. A real man. A hard-working, determined man who achieved greatness right here within our town.

The play made big statements about Jim, that was its primary aim. But it also said much about what it is possible to do in the city of Dundee.

It is true. *Smile* was just a play, only a play.

Aye, but everyone who came out of that theatre had a little more pride in their city than when they went in.

There is an enormous and a lasting value in that.

Chris Alexander was given plaudits for his portrayal of 'Jimmy' a complex role in *Smile* that was part muse, part narrator, part inner voice.

A man for all football seasons

TRIBUTE: PHIL DIFFER, SMILE AUTHOR.

OF of all the people interviewed for this book, Phil Differ had to do the best job of getting to the very core of Jim McLean as a person, how he thinks, what drives him. The essence of a man.

Phil had to put Jim on a theatre stage as a believable, accurate character, a character that his audience was going to recognise. Because a lot of people who came to see *Smile* had an opinion, an experience of Jim, even if it was just watching him on TV or in full flow at Tannadice. Phil couldn't afford to have this Dundee audience come away from it thinking: "Nah, Jim wisnae like that at a'".

This required Phil to do a lot of talking. He talked to Dundee United people, he talked to former colleagues of Jim, United's stars of the past, and also those who didn't quite make it with the club. Phil is, of course, no stranger to writing about football people, being the creator of *Only An Excuse?* The TV series that is such an important part of Scotland's Hogmanay celebrations.

Phil told me, "*Smile* is about a complex man, a man who had gravitas, but also an ever-present sense of humour, and a man who had doubts and fears. A real person. He reminded me of my dad, a very shy person.

"Jim looked uncomfortable in front of a TV camera. Though whenever he was asked a question, he always gave an honest answer and a very full answer. He was always very serious. It was very unlike watching the usual sort of TV pundit who just wants to look clever after the event. Nowadays guys are paid three million quid a year to spout useless clichés on *Match of the Day*.

"Jim would give a true assessment of how he thought a game had gone. He'd say 'this was a disgrace' or 'that was wrong' even after his team won. It was the opposite if the 'over the moon' football manager interview.

"You could see that he felt the pressure of talking to the media. But the more footage I watched, the more I learned from people, the more I felt I liked Jim. I admired him. No one else I've ever seen was so balanced and truthful when saying how their football team performed. You've got to respect that.

"And through talking to Doris and Gary, and the more I learned, I liked him even more. They told me that he laughed at Eric and Ernie, listened to Neil Diamond, the stuff all fathers like. And that he'd sing or whistle about the house. The more I discovered the more I thought he was like my father and everyone's father.

"In my head, when Doris and Gary were talking about him, I kept thinking: that's what faithers dae when gan aboot the hoose. Like mah ain faither.

"Fathers do that, don't they. But when they go out of the house, to their work, they are different.

"More than anything, and this is quite tough to say, having learned so much about Jim, one thing kept occurring to me. I wish I could have sat and just had a cuppy tea and a blether with him."

Phil well knows the illogical approach fans have to football. He knows how fans think, the things they see clearly, the blind spots they have, the wild cheers of victory, the hurtful boos of defeat, the obsessive attention to detail and jealous umbrage taken to anything that sounds remotely like criticism of their club. They are an unforgiving type of person. And that is all fans of all clubs.

A play like *Smile* couldn't have been written by a non-football person. Perhaps strange, then, that he doesn't describe *Smile* as a football play.

"It's firstly about an extraordinary man," he says. "I couldn't underestimate how loved Jim McLean is in Dundee and couldn't get away from the success he brought to the footballing community, of course. But I wanted to represent the real person behind the driven individual that anyone interested in Scottish football in the 1970s, '80s and '90s will remember.

"I didn't want to make him 'Saint Jim', I needed it to be realistic. But I kept in sight that I wanted to present a play about a human being.

"A thing Doris said really touched me. She'd spoken to me at length, and told me all about Jim. But then said, 'I wish I could ask him: was that OK what I said? Is that right?' She very much wanted it to be right too.

"It struck me what an amount of trust she'd put in me. Which was lovely, but frightening too.

■ Phil Differ. The more he learned about Jim McLean, the more he grew to like him.

SMILE AT THE REP

"After the first night, the first time Doris saw the play, I asked her 'was it OK? Did we do it right'? And she said she'd loved it. I'd been very nervous. So much so that I'd gone out and had a walk round the theatre to try to gather myself. I was wondering, 'why did I do this'!

"I loved doing it, though. It became a huge part of my life. I spent a lot of time thinking it through.

"The play is about nostalgia, a pride in the glories, but also the other side. Of looking back when a man grows older and thinks about his life. It is about reflecting on what you are, what you were, and how you became that person. I tried to show the inner thoughts of a man who sacrificed a lot of his family life for his job, and harbours regrets over that.

"And if it is about a man, then there is a lot to be considered. I knew Jim was revered in the city of Dundee and was terrified of getting him 'wrong' somehow in the fans' eyes. Of not capturing what he is. The face he showed to the football world is probably the face the fans remembered. That's what people saw. You can't get away from the football side of him.

"I have been wondering if United fans might take one thing from the play, while fans of other clubs might regard it differently? But that's what football is like, isn't it. We all see it through the prisms of our allegiances. It was a challenge to work that into the play. Scotland has a funny relationship with football. It is tender and very harsh at the same time. And we love good football played by our team but hate it played by any other team.

■ **Finn Dossing. A strapping young United "giant"!**

"The play exists within the framework of Scottish football. It has to. But I had to portray the game in a particular way. I couldn't go into blow by blow match reports to explain what Jim McLean achieved. It was a play after all, not a sports report."

I don't think Phil has anything to worry about. *Smile* is a really quite a thing to behold. It is a play of course, but a many-layered thing. It is a play in which Dundee United fans found much to make them swell with pride. That's one level. But it also did its job of looking at what it is to be a man. All the doubts, all the regrets. It is about contemplation of who you really are as a person. It is about growing old, as Phil was aiming for, and losing some parts of what you once were.

It must be added here that Phil is quite a fellah. A very clever man. He is entertaining, immensely likable, effortlessly funny and great company. You can see the stand-up comedian in him and why he is such a popular after-dinner speaker. Our 30-minute chat turned into a wide-ranging 90-minute conversation about Jim McLean, the city of Dundee, its "schemes", its self image, the mistake that is building football grounds in remote locations outside cities, the V&A, Jim Morrison and The Doors, Junior football and how best to plead innocence to the ref if accused of a raised-elbow foul.

Phil didn't mention how old he is, though I'd guess at over 21. But he still plays football. It's difficult to give up, he says. As it is for all of us.

Phil plays in a league that is supposed to be sporting and gentlemanly, but isn't quite all that. Aye, I say, I know what he means. Anyone who ever played amateur football in Scotland knows what that means. And he has always (kind of) "liked" Dundee United. None of us, who are football fans, find it easy to step away from our tribe to give much credence to what other clubs do. But Phil describes his "soft spot" for United.

"The one thing I always remember about Dundee United is the Scandinavians in the 1960s, Finn Dossing, Mogens Berg, all of them. Suddenly United exploded on to the football scene I'd known as a laddie.

"They played in all-white back then, and these Vikings looked huge. Every other player in Scotland was a wee tanner ba' sort of bloke but these Danish and Swedish guys were great big strapping giants. It is how I've always thought of United. Big strong laddies. It's funny how your mind sticks on an image of a team.

"For some reason I always liked the triangular walls at the corner flags of the old Tannadice terracing. I don't really know why, it was probably just that no other ground had anything like it. If you saw it on telly you instantly knew where the cameras were. They gave the ground character.

"And when United and Aberdeen were big and challenging in the 1980s, I always thought United were the better team to watch. And I feared that, when they were playing Celtic, that they'd do something unexpected, there was something extra in there that they'd spring on you, or pull out some great bit of football that could beat you. And I always wanted Celtic to sign Paul Sturrock, of course, he'd have done well at Celtic Park.

"When the word was that Jim McLean was going to Rangers, I thought 'aw naw, he'll turn them into a proper team'. Because he would have done. I heard Luggy being interviewed and he reckoned that if Jim had gone to Ibrox then he would have quickly signed Catholics just to make his point about who he could and couldn't sign. And that Dave Narey and himself might have been among the first ones he would have bought. Thank goad Jim didnae go to Rangers! He saw the light!

"He probably should have gone for career reasons, mind. He'd have made a success of it. But I think it was loyalty, whether to club or family or both, that made him stay at Dundee United. And, again, that tells you a lot about the man."

To end, I ask if anything surprised Phil about putting on this unique play in the city of Dundee. Typically, his answer is amusing and insightful.

"I loved that people who didn't usually go to the theatre came and said to me it was better than telly, better than the movies. I'd expected that non-theatre people would come, but their reaction still surprised me! I loved that the audience applauded at odd moments, and shouted out encouragement as well. It was a wee bit of football brought into the auditorium, and I think it was a wee bit of a shock to some people. The actors had to wait until it had finished! The audience got involved, as fans do at games, and gave it a wee bit of themselves. It made it totally unlike a normal play, but all the more wonderful for it.

"I truly loved coming to Dundee and doing this project. Jim McLean was really quite a man."

■ **Phil says that when he visited as a Celtic supporter he felt Tannadice always had "character".**

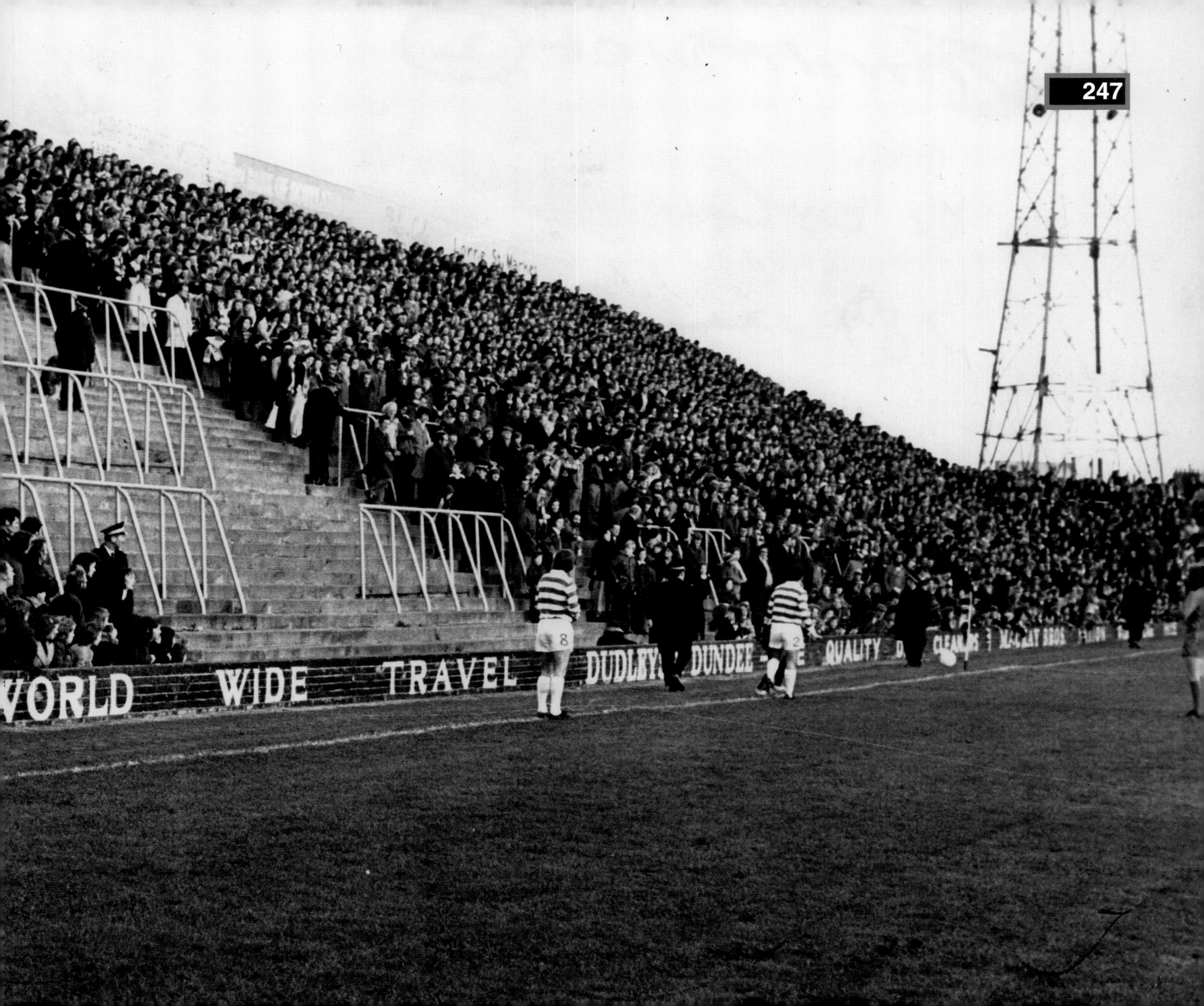
WIDE
TRAVEL
DUNDEE
QUALITY

Who am I? How will I be remembered?

TRIBUTE: BARRIE HUNTER, WHO PLAYED JIM IN SMILE

JIM MCLEAN probably hasn't ever given much thought, if any, to who would play him in a stage version of his life. Who does?

But Barrie Hunter, who played the part of Jim in *Smile* to great acclaim, had to pay forensic attention to how he portrayed the man, because he grew to understand what this man meant to the audience.

"I knew from the start that this was an unusual part to play," Barrie said. "It came with a lot of challenges. Playing a living person is very different to playing a fictional character. A high proportion of the people who came to see *Smile* had an idea of what Jim McLean looks like, what he had done, and what he is as a person.

"But I couldn't merely do an impersonation, it had to be an interpretation that captured the essence of Jim but also revealed or explained truths about him and different facets of him that only emerged over a period of years. I studied all the footage I could find, looked at all the photos. I talked to people who had stories about Jim – which wasn't hard, everyone in this area seems to have a Jim McLean anecdote.

"I looked at his speech patterns, how his mouth moved when he talked. Sally (Reid, see page 250) directed it very well, I have to say. She'd keep telling me to articulate less, to put in a few more glottal stops – the opposite, really, of how directors usually ask their actors to perform.

"I also paid a lot of attention to what Jim was like in motion. He rarely stood still. I had to look at how he walked, his mannerisms and habits. In fact I was amazed by one piece of footage. It showed Jim leaving his seat in the grandstand, running down a few stairs and stepping on to and over the perimeter wall at Tannadice to give instructions to his players. He did it all with one hand in his pocket! Who does that!

"That's the sort of thing I wanted to get right. He also had to be visually believable. We showed his tan from when he and Doris would spend time at their Florida house, his gold bracelet, the way he dressed. All of that had to be looked at. The wardrobe department bought a 1980s-era suit, and had a few extra pleats put in below the waistline. Just like suits had in those days.

"I then had to let the words of the script take me to Jim's era and to him as a person. Towards the end of the play Jim questions himself, asking: 'Who am I? How will I be remembered?' It is a highly-charged, poignant moment. He addresses the audience directly while doing this. I looked out at a sea of faces and thought that this wasn't a usual theatre crowd. There were lots of male faces who I suspected weren't habitual theatre-goers, but who were there because of the special nature of this production.

"They felt an ownership of the play, an ownership of Jim McLean as a character because they had an emotional investment in the history and personality of this man. They were watching the play but also reliving experiences from the past.

"It was made even more poignant by knowing that Jim's wife and family would be attending too. It created an intensity that made this an emotional part on several levels. I greatly enjoyed it though. It's a part I will always look back on with affection.

"And I came away with a very different regard for Jim McLean. A lot of respect and a bit more insight into a special man doing a quite incredible job. I came to appreciate his extraordinary achievements and also his overwhelming desire to never, ever let the supporters down. I grew to greatly like him, and developed a real soft spot for Dundee United and the club's fans."

■ **Barrie Hunter has played many roles in his career, but for a section of the Dundee public, people who might not usually go to the theatre, he has earned a reputation as a brilliant actor. He will always be remembered and respected as "the man who played Jim", and who did it so fantastically well.**

UNITED
DUNDEE

How dare they laugh at him?

TRIBUTE: SALLY REID, SMILE DIRECTOR.

SALLY REID directed *Smile*, which led her to regard the play in a slightly different way to most of us and to look upon Jim McLean in a different way to all of us.

For one of the performances Sally took a side-front seat at Dundee Rep and didn't watch a moment of the play. She watched the audience.

She saw grown men cry and asked herself what are they crying for? What have we done here? But she also saw men smiling, laughing and even shouting encouragement, and again asked herself: what is making them do this?

In truth, she already knew the answers. These were the reactions she intended to inspire when constructing the play. From the very start, Sally felt a sense of responsibility to firstly give her audience an entertaining evening, and show them a version of Jim McLean they recognised. But then go somewhere else entirely with it.

Sally knows football. She grew up with a father who loves the game and was a regular attender of matches. And she knew Jim McLean as a notorious figure in the game, the usual version of him. But after digging deeper, speaking to his colleagues, players, and loved ones, she found her opinion had greatly changed.

The opening scene of *Smile* had Jim explode on to the stage, ranting at a refereeing injustice. This represented the clichéd way Jim has often been portrayed. In her audience-watching, Sally was slightly angry during this part of the performance because she felt people might be laughing at Jim (though, of course, this is the desired result of this section of the play). But Sally had grown to feel so protective of Jim that she almost resented the fact that her intention had worked so well.

How dare people laugh at Jim? Or assume they knew a man because they were seeing this singular version of him that had been described so often in the media?

From this start, the play took Jim on quite a journey.

Jim was shown to intend everything, every single action he took, to be for the good of the club. He phoned players' digs on a Friday night to ensure they'd be in tip-top condition for the next day's game. He fined players for not being entertaining enough – because he truly wanted the fans to feel entertained.

Portraying these things required Sally to know her subject extremely well. But you can't get under the skin of a stranger ,so Sally had to understand Jim McLean at an inner-workings level. Along with writer Phil, she talked at great length to those who knew him.

Armed with this, Sally found ways to show that Jim was often a very funny man, with a witty turn of phrase. She showed Jim contemplating the things he has learned over the years, and had him talking to the audience – the

Sally grew protective of Jim.

audience sometimes taking the part of players, sometimes asked to sit in judgment of Jim, sometimes as the object of his wrath, sometimes confronted with poignant questions.

Chris Alexander as Jimmy, who was in turn an interviewer, one of Jim's players, the voice of Jim's younger (or older) self, or the voice of the football-obsessive, played a complicated role to perfection. And Barrie Hunter (a pages back in this book) gave a sharp and nuanced performance as Jim.

The result of all this was powerful. *Smile* deserves an audience outwith Dundee. It contains an examination of a cultural phenomenon – the hold that football has on a part of society and how it affects many people's mentality. But it also contains a measure of a man, a look at the human condition.

The final scenes of *Smile* were the most touching. Sally and writer Phil devised and delivered subtle messages.

When Jim faced the audience and asked "Who am I? Where am I?" it was a question asked by a man who wondered where all his care and obsession with football had led him, but was also a reference to the condition Jim finds himself in with his condition.

The release of balloons, which might have looked somewhat incongruous, represented that Jim will still react to and play keepie-up with a balloon, even if only with his hands. His footballer's timing and sense of where gravity will make a ball (or balloon) fall isn't lost.

Anyone who has ever had a relative suffering in this way will recognise this. Shadows of former personality traits, and ghosts of old habits, often show themselves.

Sally directed a play about a remarkable man, but also about a man growing old as all of us grow old. And falling ill, as many of us do in our later years. She showed us something about Jim McLean and also suggested things to us about ourselves.

The result was a moving, thought-provoking, multi-layered piece of art that did Jim justice, and presented the city of Dundee in a new light.

Jim achieved great things with Dundee United, he always did his best for the city of Dundee.

He was also a remarkable and complicated man. One who always did his family, and the supporters, proud.

Pics courtesy of Dundee Rep.

DUNDEE
UNITED

Jim made United 'the world famous'

ANALYSIS: STEVE FINAN.

DUNDEE UNITED supporters sometimes like to use the words "the world famous" before saying Dundee United. There is humour in it, sometimes it's intended with a little irony – but there is a ring of seriousness too. We think the club is special.

But then every club's supporters say that.

We like to think that we're not like other clubs, that there is something just that little bit extra about going to Tannadice, wearing tangerine colours. We reckon that we share a special bond with each other, that we've seen a lot, that we've suffered a lot, but that we just keep coming back, stronger, bigger, better, and there are more and more of us all the time.

But then every club's supporters think that they're not like those of other clubs.

So this confidence requires a bit of history to give it context. United came from nothing. It is a classic rags to riches story. The tale of a club from a football backwater that spent the first 50 years of its existence as a deeply unfashionable outfit, unsuccessful, largely ignored, not much to say for itself.

Scottish football is horribly static. Since unseating Queen's Park, Rangers and Celtic have held power for nigh on a century and a half. The likes of Hearts, Hibs and Aberdeen grab a cup or a championship from time to time, with St Mirren, Killie, Hamilton, St Johnstone, Partick, Motherwell, and Dundee further out on the periphery of success. The rest have had but brief moments in the sun.

In recent years, Inverness and Ross County have made it to the top league, and won trophies. But their crowds remain low, their small stadiums count against them being seen as truly big boys, yet. Gretna had a run a few years ago, but their artificial bubble soon burst.

The fundamental make-up of Scottish football rarely changes in a significant way.

Apart from Dundee United.

There is something truly romantic about United. No other club has dragged itself up from being one that routinely finished around the bottom of the Second Division (the lowest it was possible to go at the time).

Without any helping hand, without a Russian oligarch or Middle-Eastern oil money, United forced a way to a seat at the rich man's table.

United now have the stadium, the support, the trophies, and the European reputation of being a big Scottish club.

All of this has been achieved since 1960, when Jerry Kerr, and it must be fully acknowledged a quite brilliant group of men serving as directors, stepped up to the First Division and laid the foundations for further growth.

Then Jim McLean became manager.

That's the difference, the thing other clubs don't have in their history. That's why United became world famous.

The word charisma doesn't appear anywhere else in this book. I have saved it for this end-piece. Because above everything else, Jim McLean had a charisma. He possessed a force of personality, a strength of character that demanded the utmost effort from his players, his board of directors, and his club's fans.

Jim forced Dundee United to become a top-six club. Ever since he became manager (and even when not playing like a top-six team on the park) the club has had the reputation, the standing in the game, to be continually referred to as one of Scotland's top clubs.

Jim McLean did that. He would be embarrassed by this accolade, and would be the first to reel off dozens of names of those who also worked very hard, who were also brilliant at their jobs. And he'd be right to do that.

But Jim was the leader.

That's why there is a statue to him. That's why there was a play written about him. That's why there is this book full of tributes to him.

Jim will be remembered at our club, for all time, as he is in the photo on the right. A champion.

He is, and will always remain:

JIM McLEAN DUNDEE UNITED LEGEND

Thank you

To all Dundee United supporters past, present and future.

To all the players, celebrities, and fans who kindly contributed articles to this book.

To: John Alexander for sponsoring this book, and Adele Pearson's role in making that happen.

To: Tom Duthie.

Stewart Weir.

Leon Strachan.

Dave Martin, Fotopress.

Stewart Alexander.

Grant Millar.

Rachel Falconer.

James Kirk.

Craig Houston.

Gill Martin.

Sylwia Jackowska.

Jacqui Hunter.

David Powell.

Barry Sullivan.

Irina Florian.

Kirsty Smith.

Gary Thomas.

Duncan Laird.

Raymond Barr.

Seher Sultan.

Brendan Malone.

Tom Cairns.

Graeme Strachan.

Calum Woodger.

Graeme Finnan.

George Cran.

Carole Finan.

Rebecca Finan.

Lewis Finan.

Fraser T. Ogilvie.

To Doris, Colin and Gary McLean.

Most of all, thank you to Jim McLean himself. It was a hell of a ride, Jim. We will never forget.

If you liked this book, you'll love these too

ARABS AWAY THERE'S NEVER BEEN A FOOTBALL BOOK LIKE THIS. IT ISN'T ABOUT FOOTBALL. IT'S ABOUT YOU

Just £12.99 with FREE P&P

PRODUCTION OF THIS BOOK WAS SPONSORED BY: